Speaking Our LANGUAGE

Fàilte! *Welcome to the first* **Speaking Our Language** *study pack.*

Speaking Our Language has been specially designed to teach conversational Gaelic in a lively and friendly way. That's why you'll find cartoons, puzzles and news items alongside the grammar and language exercises. Most importantly, you'll be encouraged to practise your Gaelic in everyday situations with your family and friends.

Further help is available too. On page 72, you'll find details of the Speaking Our Language audio tapes and videos, and the new information service linked to the project.

We're sure you'll enjoy learning Gaelic with Speaking Our Language…

Gur math a thèid leibh – *Good Luck!*

Margaret MacDonald   **Project Co-ordinator**, Cànan

Scripts: Dr. Richard Cox
Language Consultants:
Boyd Robertson, Catriona Campbell, Jordanhill College of Education
Contributors: Seonag Barbour, Ian MacDonald
Project Consultants: ACEN / S4C
Cartoons: Andy Petrie
Graphic Design: Margo Dick, Cànan.

Printed by Highland Printers, Inverness

ISBN 1-897873-00-X

Clàr
CONTENTS

Duilleag
PAGE

A Ceum air Cheum 2
Step by step

B Oisean an Teaghlaich 39
Family corner

C Aig an Taigh 46
At home

D Cò, Ciamar, Càite? 55
Who, how and where?

E Dibhearsain 64
Time to relax
Nursery rhymes – Songs – Crossword – 'Alba'

F A bheil thu a' tuigsinn? 68
Do you understand?

Ciamar a tha an cànan 69
ag obrachadh?
How does the language work?

A' Bruidhinn Ar Cànain 72
Speaking Our Language

This project has been supported by:

Iomairt An Eilein
Sgitheanaich & Loch Aillse
Skye & Lochalsh
ENTERPRISE

Highlands & Islands
ENTERPRISE

Speaking Our Language is a Scottish Television Production funded by

● **C**omataidh **T**elebhisein **G**àidhlig ●

Published and Distributed by

Sabhal Mòr Ostaig, Isle of Skye IV44 8RQ
Tel: 04714 345

Thanks also to the following: Borders Regional Council, Craig & Lindsay Campbell, Terry Evans, Willie Fraser, Glasgow District Council, Invergordon Distillers Group, William McGonagle, Polly MacInnes, Alisdair Mackinnon, Janet MacLeod, Praban na Linne Ltd., Elen Rhys, SALT, Alistair Scott Photography, Vicky Siegfried, and to the many other individuals and organisations who contributed to this pack.

Sounding good in Gaelic
Blas math air a' Ghàidhlig

Many sounds in Gaelic are similar to English ones. Letters are sometimes used in different ways in Gaelic, but there are not many sounds that are completely unfamiliar. Here is a round up of some useful points.

We've given some help with how to say words when they first appear by putting the approximate English sounds in *italics* in brackets.

THE LONG AND THE SHORT OF IT

If there's an accent (eg. à or è) on a vowel, it makes the sound longer:

càr *(kaahr)* – a car
car *(kahr)* – a turn or twist

bàta *(baahtuh)* – a boat
bata *(bahtuh)* – a walking stick

BEWARE OF SILENT LETTERS

Groups of letters may be silent, especially in the middle of a word:

Giogha *(Gyee-ah)* – Gigha
Uibhist *(Uhy-ishtch)* – Uist

and at the end of a word:

cèilidh *(kaylee)* – a ceilidh

THE TROUBLE WITH 'H'

The letter h is used at the start of a word, as in English hello…

Hallò!

NA HEARADH

…but much more frequently with other letters:

bh is like an English v, as in van.

ch is pronounced like the ch in loch.

dh or **gh** is either pronounced like a gargled g, or like the y of yellow.

fh is silent. Very occasionally it is pronounced like h in hello – we'll let you know when!

mh is like the v in van.

ph is an f sound, as in phone.

sh or **th** is either an h sound, as in house, or like the h of house and the y of yellow together.

SOUNDS DIFFERENT

As in other languages, people may speak differently because of where they come from. Don't let this worry you! It is good practice to copy others when learning a language, so if you know people who speak Gaelic you could copy them.

Greeting someone
A' cur fàilte air cuideigin

ASKING HOW SOMEONE IS

ciamar a tha sibh?
(kaymuhr uh ha shiv)
how are you?
The '**c**' of **ciamar** sounds very like the '**c**' of **cute**.

HELLO!

hallò *(hallo)* is very common

hai *(hi)* is more informal

SAYING HOW YOU ARE

tha gu math *(ha guh mah)* – fine

glè mhath *(glay vah)* – very well

Think of the name of this whisky liqueur – it comes from Gaelic

chan eil dona *(cha nyehl dawhnuh)* – not bad

THANK YOU

tapadh leibh *(tahpuh leeve)* – thank you

People often use **tapadh leibh** when they answer.

RETURNING THE COMPLIMENT

ciamar a tha sibh fèin? *(fayn)*
How are you?

JUMBLED ANSWERS

The players in this word game are trying to finish in one go. Order the letters so they give an answer to the greeting '**ciamar a tha sibh?**'

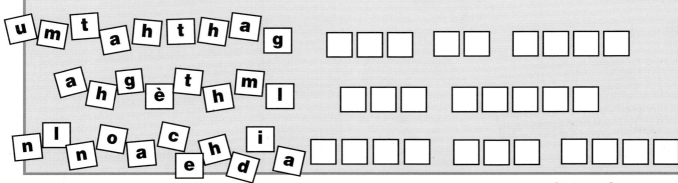

Answers: 1. tha gu math, 2. glè mhath, 3. chan eil dona

Greeting someone
A' cur fàilte air cuideigin

GREETING PEOPLE THROUGH THE DAY

madainn mhath (*mahteen vah*) – good morning

feasgar math (*fayskuhr mah*) –
good afternoon or good evening

latha math (*lahuh mah*) – good day

You may also hear people say:

madainn mhath dhuibh (*ghuhyv*) –
good morning to you, or

feasgar math dhuibh – good afternoon or good
evening to you.

Feasgar math!

TALKING TO A CHILD OR A FRIEND

There are two words for 'you' in Gaelic:

sibh and **thu** (*oo*).

Thu is used when speaking to a close friend or a child.

Sibh is more formal. It is used
when talking to someone older
than you, or to someone in
authority. It is also used when
talking to more than one
person. If you are in doubt
about which to use, stick to
sibh.

Ciamar a
tha thu?

SAYING THANK YOU

tapadh leibh is used along
with **sibh**.

tapadh leat (*tahpuh leht*)
is used along with **thu**.

Tapadh leat.

EAVESDROPPING

You are sightseeing on your own for the day, and can't
help overhearing conversations from time to time. Can
you tell what time of day it is, and how the speakers
are feeling?

Màiri: **Hallò, madainn mhath!**

Iain: **Madainn mhath!**

Màiri: **Ciamar a tha sibh?**

Iain: **Tha gu math, tapadh leibh.**

_____

Mòrag: **Hai, feasgar math!**

Alasdair: **Feasgar math! Ciamar a tha sibh?**

Mòrag: **Och! Chan eil dona.**

_____

Pàdraig: **Latha math! Ciamar a tha sibh?**

Calum: **Glè mhath, tapadh leibh. Ciamar a
tha sibh fèin?**

Pàdraig: **Tha gu math.**

_____

A' cur fàilte air cuideigin

TALKING ABOUT THE WEATHER

People often comment on the weather when they meet.

tha i brèagha... *(ha ee breea-uh)* – it's lovely...

tha i blàth... *(blaah)* –it's warm...

tha i fliuch... *(flewch)* – it's wet...

tha i fuar... *(foouhr)* – it's cold...

...an-diugh
(uhn joob) – today

...nach eil?
(nach ayl) – isn't it?

To agree with someone when they comment on the weather:

tha or
tha, tha i brèagha for example.

(Some dialects use **tha e...** instead of **tha i...**)

> Tha i fliuch an-diugh, nach eil?

> Tha!

ALL RIGHT ON THE NIGHT!

Tonight is your big chance to star in a play, but you find the script is blotched with coffee stains!
To be word perfect, you'll have to fill in the gaps.

WISH YOU WERE HERE...

Make a comment on the weather in each of these pictures. The first has been completed for you.

1. **Tha i brèagha an-diugh, nach eil?**

2. ....
   ....
   ....

3. ....
   ....

4. ....
   ....
   ....

Clumsy Fearghas enters the laundrette, where Iseabail is filing her nails:

Fearghas: **Madainn mhath, Iseabail!**

Iseabail: **Madainn mhath?** (She looks at her watch) **Feasgar ....!**

Fearghas: (Apologetically) **Feasgar math. Ciamar a......... sibh?**

Iseabail: **Chan eil .....** (Grudgingly) **Ciamar a tha sibh.........?**

Fearghas: **Tha gu math, ...leibh.**

(Handsome Niall enters)

Fearghas & Niall to each other: **.......... a tha sibh?**

Iseabail: (Pretending indifference) **Tha i brèagha an-diugh, ... eil?**

Giving your name
Ag innse d' ainm

SAYING WHO YOU ARE

Introduce yourself by saying:

is mise... *(iss mishuh)* – I am

Hallò. Is mise Calum MacLeòid.

Is mise Màiri NicLeòid.

Hallò. Is mise Mòrag NicAsgaill.

MAC IN SURNAMES

If you are female you use **Nic** *(neechk)* instead of **Mac** *(machk)* :

Iain MacLeòid – John MacLeod
but
Sìne NicLeòid – Jean MacLeod

Seumas MacAsgaill – James MacAskill
but
Anna NicAsgaill – Ann MacAskill

There is more about surnames in the 'Cò, ciamar, càite?' section.

Madainn mhath. Is mise Ailean MacAsgaill.

Madainn mhath. Thig a-steach.

Here the salesman is asked to come in –
thig a-steach *(heek uh-styehch)*

You have been invited to go to a party by a friend. People are very friendly and introduce themselves to you. Introduce yourself to them:

Feasgar math. Is mise Catrìona.

Hallò. Is mise Iain.

Hallò. Is mise Anna. Ciamar a tha sibh?

Feasgar math, a Chatrìona.
Is mise ....
....

Hallò, Iain.
....
....

Hallò, Anna.
....
....

Giving your name
Ag innse d' ainm

ASKING SOMEONE'S NAME

To ask someone's name, you say

dè an t-ainm a th' oirbh?

    (jay uhn tehnehm uh huhruv) –
what's your name?

To reply, just give your name.

Dè an t-ainm a th' oirbh?

Sìne NicLeòid.

Dè an t-ainm a th' oirbh?

Alasdair Cambeul.

FILLING IN FORMS

If you are asked your name on a Gaelic form you will certainly see the word **ainm** *(ehnehm)*; but you may also come across the following:

ainm[ean] baistidh *(ehnehm[uhn] bashchee)* – Christian name[s]

cinneadh *(keenyugh)* – surname

(In some dialects, **sloinneadh** *(sluhnyugh)* is the word used for surname.)

litrichean mòra *(leehtreechun more-uh)* – capital letters

An Comunn Gaidhealach
(The Highland Association)

Ainm.................................

COMANN AN LUCHD – IONNSACHAIDH
(a learners' society)

IARRTAS BALLRACHD
(membership form)

Ainm baistidh: ....

Cinneadh ....

Gairm

(a Gaelic magazine)

Ainm ....
(Litrichean Mòra)

Nah-Arainnich
(a Gaelic club)

Bliadhna 19..–19..

Ainm: ....

INTRODUCING SOMEONE ELSE

This can be done using one word:

seo... (*shawh*) – this is… or here is…

seo Iain – this is John

seo Iain agus Niall – this is John and Neil

agus (*ahghuhs*) – and

WHO'S WHO?

Some phrases which could be useful:

an duine agam (*uhn duhnyuh ackuhm*) – my husband

a' bhean agam (*uh vehn*) – my wife

an nighean agam (*uhn nyeeuhn*) – my daughter

am mac agam (*uhm machk*) – my son

an caraid agam (*uhn kareetch*) – my friend

WHO'S DOING THE TALKING?

Fill in the introductions for these speakers:

Seo ....

....

....

....

SAY THAT AGAIN?

How much do you remember so far? Use a piece of paper to cover these phrases. Move the paper down a little to show the first phrase in the left hand column, and try to say the phrase in Gaelic. Move the paper down to reveal the correct Gaelic phrase on the right.

How are you?	
Fine, thanks	**Ciamar a tha sibh?**
Good afternoon	**Tha gu math, tapadh leibh**
It's a lovely day	**Feasgar math**
I'm John Campbell	**Tha i brèagha an-diugh**
This is Anne	**Is mise Iain Caimbeul**
This is my wife, Mary	**Seo Anna**
This is my son	**Seo a' bhean agam, Màiri**
What's your name?	**Seo am mac agam**
	Dè an t-ainm a th' oirbh?

This page is linked to • TV Programme 2 • Audio Cassette 1

Giving your address
Ag innse do sheòladh

Saying where you live

To say 'I live' or 'I stay', use

tha mi a' fuireach... *(ha me uh foohruch)* – I live…

...ann an Sruighlea *(ahwn uhn Sruhyli)* –
…in Stirling

...ann an Obar Dheathain *(Ohpur-ehihn)* –
…in Aberdeen

...ann an Dùn Dèagh *(Doohn Jay)* – …in Dundee

Watch out for placenames beginning in b, m, and p – where **ann am** is used for 'in'.

...ann am Muile *(ahwn uhm Moohluh)* –
…in Mull

...ann am Baile Ghobhainn *(Bahluh Ghoheen)* –
…in Govan

...ann am Pàislig *(Paashleek)* – …in Paisley

Spot the Match

A visitor to Scotland has bought a Gaelic map and has asked you to help interpret it. Match these Gaelic name with their equivalents. Use the map for clues.

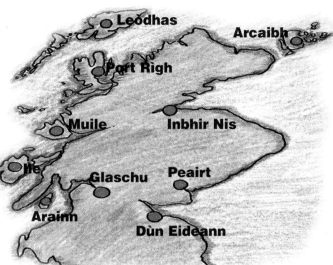

Leòdhas *(Lyewuhs)*	Islay
Port Rìgh *(Pawrstree)*	Perth
Muile *(Moohluh)*	Edinburgh
Ìle *(Eeluh)*	Arran
Arainn *(Ahreen)*	Lewis
Peairt *(Pehrshch)*	Portree
Arcaibh *(Ahrkuhv)*	Glasgow
Inbhir Nis *(Eenuhrneesh)*	Mull
Glaschu *(Glahsuhchooh)*	Inverness
Dùn Eideann *(Doohnaychuhn)*	Orkney

Moving House

These people have moved house. Take the part of each one in turn to say who you are and where you live. The first one is written out for you.

9

GIVING MORE DETAILS

One of these phrases might be useful:

anns a' bhaile *(ahwns uh vahluh)* – in town or
in the town
(Note that **baile** can mean a town or a village.)

ann am meadhan a' bhaile
(ahwn uhm mee-ahn uh vahluh) –
in the town centre

Meadhan
a' Bhaile
Village
centre

faisg air a' bhaile *(fahshk ayhr uh vahlah)* –
near town or near the town

air an dùthaich *(ayhr uhn dooheech)* –
in the country

NAMING YOUR STREET

The following are often seen and used:

sràid *(sraahtch)* – street

rathad *(rahuht)* – road

ionad *(eehnuht)* – place

BANK STREET
SRAID A' BHANCA

An Rathad Ard
High Road

Ionad na Margaidh
Market Place

DUNVEGAN ROAD
Rathad Dhùn Bheagain

LINK UP THE FACTS

You have been asked to suggest some ideas for new characters in a television drama series. From the information pack you have been sent, link up the facts you think best suit the actors that have been asked to take part. For each of the characters, choose a name, location, a road or street name, and the type of accommodation they live in.

taigh

Seonag NicAsgaill

bungalo

Eilidh Chaimbeul

flat

air an dùthaich

anns a' bhaile

carabhan

Rathad an Loch

Ailean MacLeòid

ann am meadhan a' bhaile

Sràid na h-Eaglaise

Sràid a' Bhanca

BANCA NA H-ALBA

faisg air a' bhaile

Giving your address
Ag innse do sheòladh

ainm: ....

ainm sràide: ....

....

seòrsa togalaich: ....
(type of accommodation)

....

àite: ....
(location)

ainm: ....

ainm sràide: ....

....

seòrsa togalaich: ....
(type of accommodation)

....

àite: ....
(location)

Rathad na Beinne

ainm: ....

ainm sràide: ....

....

seòrsa togalaich: ....
(type of accommodation)

....

àite: ....
(location)

Niall Moireasdan

ainm: ....

ainm sràide: ....

....

seòrsa togalaich: ....
(type of accomodation)

....

àite: ....
(location)

ASKING WHERE SOMEONE LIVES

If you want to ask someone where they live, use

càit a bheil sibh a' fuireach?
(kaatch uh vayhl shiv uh foohruch) –
where do you live?

If talking to a child, use **thu**

càit a bheil thu a' fuireach?

RETURN TO SENDER

You have found a letter and a bundle of photographs on the bus and want to return them to the owner. There is no address at the top of the letter, but it might contain information about where the writer lives. Here's the first part of the letter. You may not understand all of it first time, but have a go! Try and find the facts asked for in the box.

> Iain, a charaid,
>
> Ciamar a tha thu? Tha mi fhìn glè mhath. Tha Inbhir Nis brèagha, agus tha mi a' fuireach ann am meadhan a' bhaile air Sràid a' Chaisteil. Ach tha i fuar ann an Inbhir Nis!
>
> Ciamar a tha Anna?

baile: ....

àite anns a' bhaile / location in town**:**

....

ainm sràide: ....

VOCABULARY

Iain, a charaid *(Eeahyn uh chahreetch)* – Dear John

It is very common to use **a charaid** on its own at the start of a formal letter.

tha mi fhìn glè mhath – I am very well
(heehn)

Sràid a' Chaisteil *(uh Chahshchehl)* – Castle Street

ach *(ahch)* – but

GIVING YOUR HOUSE OR PHONE NUMBER

If you're asked for your address you may have to give a house number.

ONE TO TEN

1 – 10 are fairly straightforward:

1 **aon** (*aohn*)
2 **dhà** (*ghaa*)
3 **trì** (*tree*)
4 **ceithir** (*kayhuhr*)
5 **còig** (*kohyk*)
6 **sia** (*sheeah*)
7 **seachd** (*shehchk*)
8 **ochd** (*awchk*)
9 **naoi** (*nuhy*)
10 **deich** (*juhych*)

FOR THE PHONE

Another number which will come in handy is

0 **neoni** (*nehwnee*) – nothing or zero

Port Rìgh trì seachd neoni ceithir.

COUNTING

When counting, people often stick an **a** (*uh*) on the beginning. Think of the countdown in wrestling! Before a number beginning with a vowel, **a h–** is used:

a h–aon, a dhà, a trì, a ceithir, a còig, a sia, a seachd, a h–ochd, a naoi

a h-aon, a dhà, a trì...

IN THE TEENS

If you live in a long road or street, you may need a number higher than ten. For eleven to nineteen, just use the basic number followed by **deug**:

11 **aon deug** (*aohn jeeuhk*)
12 **dhà dheug** – watch out for twelve!
    dhà <u>dh</u>eug (*ghaa yeeuhk*)
13 **trì deug** (*tree jeeuhk*)
14 **ceithir deug**
15 **còig deug**
16 **sia deug**
17 **seachd deug**
18 **ochd deug**
19 **naoi deug**

TWENTY PLUS

The traditional Gaelic system counts in blocks of twenties (like the old English form three score and ten, instead of seventy).

20 **fichead** (*feechuht*)
40 **dà fhichead** – watch out for the change in **fichead** here: **dà <u>fh</u>ichead** (*daa eechuht*)
60 **trì fichead** (*tree feechuht*)
80 **ceithir fichead**

For the numbers in between, you add 1 – 19 after **fichead**:

21 **fichead 's a naoi** – twenty and nine
31 **fichead 's a h–aon deug** – twenty and eleven
49 **dà fhichead 's a naoi** – forty and nine
65 **trì fichead 's a còig** – sixty and five
73 **trì fichead 's a trì deug** – sixty and thirteen
99 **ceithir fichead 's a naoi deug** – eighty and nineteen

's is short for **agus** – and

A HUNDRED PLUS

Ceud (*ceud*) is the word for hundred (100), but if your house number is in the hundreds just use the basic figures:

169 **aon sia naoi**
238 **dhà trì ochd**
475 **ceithir seachd còig**

ASKING SOMEONE'S ADDRESS AND PHONE NUMBER

If you want to ask someone their address, you say

dè an seòladh a th' agaibh?

> *(jay uhn shawhlugh uh hackuhv?)* – what's your address?

And for their phone number, you say

dè an àireamh fòn a th' agaibh?

> *(jay uhn aahruhv foehn uh hackuhv)* – what's your phone number?

When speaking to a child, use **agad** *(ackuht)* instead of **agaibh**:

dè an seòladh a th' agad?

dè an àireamh fòn a th' agad?

> Dè an seòladh a th' agad?

> 10, An Rathad Ard.

THE DECIMAL SYSTEM

A new system which counts in tens has been introduced and is being used mostly in schools. Counting from one to twenty–nine stays the same, but there are new words for thirty, forty, and so on.

30	**trìthead**	*(treehuht)*
31	**trìthead 's a h–aon**	*(treehuht suh haohn)*
40	**ceathrad**	*(kehruht)*
45	**ceathrad 's a còig**	*(kehruht suh kohyk)*
50	**caogad**	*(kaohkuht)*
52	**caogad 's a dhà**	*(kaohkuht suh ghaa)*
60	**seasgad**	*(shehskuht)*
70	**seachdad**	*(shehchkuht)*
77	**seachdad 's a seachd**	*(shehchkuht suh shehchk)*
80	**ochdad**	*(awchkuht)*
90	**naochad**	*(naohchuht)*

NUMBER PRACTICE

In this week's radio request programme (**Na Dùrachdan**), several of the addresses given will have house numbers. How will they be said in words? Write out the Gaelic words in full.

12 ....

17 ....

21 ....

31 ....

264 ....

Leabhar fòn   Phone book

Fill in the names, addresses and phone numbers of people you contact regularly. Use the Gaelic words for numbers and any words like road and street.

ainm: ....

seòladh: ....

....

àireamh fòn: ....

ainm: ....

seòladh: ....

....

àireamh fòn: ....

ainm: ....

seòladh: ....

....

àireamh fòn: ....

ainm: ....

seòladh: ....

....

àireamh fòn: ....

Tha gu leòr.

A bheil Gàidhlig agad?

Tha, beagan.

SAYING THAT YOU SPEAK A LANGUAGE

tha ... agam – I speak...

Gàidhlig (*Gaahlick*) – Gaelic

Beurla (*Bayhrluh*) – English

tha Gàidhlig agam – I speak Gaelic, or
I can speak Gaelic

tha Beurla agam – I speak English

SAYING THAT YOU UNDERSTAND

tha mi a' tuigsinn (*ha me uh tuhykshin*) –
I understand

ASKING SOMEONE WHETHER THEY SPEAK A LANGUAGE

a bheil ... agaibh? – do you speak...?

a bheil Gàidhlig agaibh? – do you speak Gaelic?

tha, tha Gàidhlig agam – yes, I speak Gaelic

Talking to a child you would use

a bheil Gàidhlig agad? – do you speak Gaelic?

APPLYING FOR A JOB

You are applying for a job in a busy tourist hotel.
Say that you can speak or understand these
languages.

Gàidhlig

Beurla

Albais (*Ahlahbeesh*) – Scots

Fraingis (*Fryngeesh*) – French

Gearmailtis (*Gehrehmehlteesh*) – German

Spàinntis (*Spaahynteesh*) – Spanish

....

....

....

....

TALKING ABOUT FLUENCY

The following replies will be useful:

tha, beagan (*ha bayhkahn*) – yes, a little

tha, gu leòr (*ha guh lyewhr*) – yes, plenty

and

tha mi ag ionnsachadh... (*ha me uk yuhnsuchugh*)
– I'm learning...

tha mi fileanta (*ha me feehlahntuh*) – I'm fluent

ASKING SOMEONE WHERE THEY COME FROM

cò às a tha sibh? *(koe ahs uh ha shiv)* – where are you from?

And to return the question, say

cò às a tha sibh fèin? – where are <u>you</u> from?

To a child you would use

cò às a tha thu? – where are you from?

SAYING WHERE YOU ARE FROM

To answer the question **cò às a tha sibh?**, you can just give the name of the place. However, it is more common to put **à** or **às** in front of the placename. Notice that you always use the **às** form if the Gaelic placename begins with **a'** or **an**.
eg. **à Sasainn, à Canada** but
às an Fhraing, às a' Ghearmailt.

Alba *(Ahlahbuh)*

Eirinn *(Ayhreen)*

Sasainn *(Sahseen)*

a' Chuimrigh *(uh Chuhymeree)*

an Fhraing *(uhn Rahyng)*

a' Ghearmailt *(uh Ghehrehmehlch)*

Ameireaga *(Ahmayhruhka)*

Canada *(Kahnadah)*

IDENTIFYING THE COUNTRY

For an international film festival in Inverness, you have been asked to prepare name cards for some of the countries being represented. Write each of the names against the appropriate flag.

Ask the visitors where they are from, using the question **cò às a tha sibh?**

15

A' bruidhinn mu chànanan agus cò às a tha thu

GETTING THROUGH AN INTERVIEW

These people are applying for a job in an export company with links with Cape Breton in Canada. Read each job application (**iarrtas obrach**) and then take the part of one of the candidates in the interview.

IARRTAS OBRACH

ainm: *Niall Moireasdan*

seòladh: *5 Sràid a' Bhanca, Peairt*

àireamh fòn: *Peairt 40679*

àite breith (place of birth): *Barraigh*

cànanan (languages): *Gàidhlig (fileanta), Beurla (fileanta), Fraingis (beagan), Spàinntis (ag ionnsachadh)*

IARRTAS OBRACH

ainm: *Sìne NicAmhlaigh*

seòladh: *15 An Rathad Àrd, Sruighlea*

àireamh fòn: *Sruighlea 62148*

àite breith (place of birth): *Muile*

cànanan (languages): *Gàidhlig (fileanta), Beurla (fileanta), Fraingis (ag ionnsachadh), Gearmailtis (beagan)*

Why not try the other one too?

Interviewer: **Latha math.**	Interviewer: **Latha math.**
Interviewee:	Interviewee: ....
Interviewer: **Dè an t–ainm a th' oirbh?**	Interviewer: **Dè an t–ainm a th' oirbh?**
Interviewee:	Interviewee: ....
Interviewer: **Cò às a tha sibh?**	Interviewer: **Cò às a tha sibh?**
Interviewee:	Interviewee: ....
Interviewer: **Dè an seòladh a th' agaibh?**	Interviewer: **Dè an seòladh a th' agaibh?**
Interviewee:	Interviewee: ....
Interviewer: **Dè an àireamh fòn a th' agaibh?**	Interviewer: **Dè an àireamh fòn a th' agaibh?**
Interviewee:	Interviewee: ....
Interviewer: **A bheil Gàidhlig agaibh?**	Interviewer: **A bheil Gàidhlig agaibh?**
Interviewee:	Interviewee: ....
Interviewer: **A bheil Beurla agaibh?**	Interviewer: **A bheil Beurla agaibh?**
Interviewee:	Interviewee: ....
Interviewer: **A bheil Spàinntis agaibh?**	Interviewer: **A bheil Fraingis agaibh?**
Interviewee:	Interviewee: ....
Interviewer: **A bheil Fraingis agaibh?**	Interviewer: **A bheil Gearmailtis agaibh?**
Interviewee:	Interviewee: ....

Asking for drinks

ASKING FOR A DRINK

The word for coffee is

cofaidh (*kawhfee*)

The easiest way to ask for a cup of coffee is

cofaidh, mas e ur toil e (*mahs eh uhr tawhl eh*) –
coffee, please

A fuller translation of **mas e ur toil e** would be if you
please.

You could also ask for

tì (*tee*) – tea

seoclaid (*shawhklehtsh*) – chocolate

sùgh orains (*sooh awhrinsh*) – orange juice

(You may also hear **teatha** (*tayuh*) for tea.)

SAYING PLEASE TO CLOSE FRIENDS OR CHILDREN

Instead of **mas e ur toil e,** people use **mas e do
thoil e** (*mahs eh doh hawhl eh*) for please when
talking to friends or to children.

Mas e do
thoil e!

TWO OF SOMETHING

Earlier we saw that to say the number 2 on its own, **dhà**
is used:

aon, dhà, trì – one, two, three

To say two of something, people say **dà** followed by the
word. Notice that **dà** can change the sound of the
following word. For example, **cupa** (*koohpuh*) – a cup
becomes **chupa**:

dà chupa (*daa choohpuh*) – two cups

dà chofaidh (*daa chawfee*) – two coffees

dà thì (*daa hee*) – two teas

dà shùgh orains (*daa hooh awhrinsh*) –
two orange juices

ORDERING DRINKS

The following people are dying of thirst. Order the
drinks that they have in mind – and remember to say
please!

BEING MORE PRECISE

To get exactly what you want, and to avoid awkward questions, it's a good idea to be as precise as you can when ordering:

dubh *(dooh)* – black
geal *(gyehl)* – white

cofaidh dubh – black coffee

cofaidh geal – white coffee

Notice that **tì** changes the sound of the word following:

tì dhubh *(dhooh)* – black tea

tì gheal *(yehl)* – white tea

SUGAR AND MILK?

Instead of saying white tea or white coffee, you could also say tea with milk or coffee with milk:

le bainne *(leh bahnyuh)* – with milk

tì le bainne – tea with milk

cofaidh le bainne – coffee with milk

To add sugar, use

le siùcar *(leh shoohckuhr)* – with sugar

cofaidh le siùcar – coffee with sugar

or without

gun bhainne *(guhn vahnyuh)* – without milk

gun siùcar – without sugar

gun bhainne is gun siùcar – without milk or sugar (Literally, and without sugar – **is** is a short form of **agus**)

tì gun siùcar – tea without sugar

[In some dialects **bainne** is pronounced like *bohnyuh*.]

SERVING THE DRINKS

cofaidh geal dhuibh – white coffee for you

Use **dhuibh** in the same situations where you would use **sibh** (notice the bhs!). You'd use **dhut** *(ghooht)* to a close friend or child:

sùgh orains dhut – an orange juice for you

THREE OR MORE OF SOMETHING

Instead of saying three coffees, four teas, people say three cups of coffee, four cups of tea:

trì cupannan *(koohpuhnuhn)* **cofaidh** – three cups of coffee

trì cupannan tì – three cups of tea

ceithir cupannan cofaidh – four cups of coffee

ceithir cupannan tì – four cups of tea

THE SAME AGAIN

You're in a coffee shop and are going to order another round of drinks. The note of the first round was in English, but the assistant can speak Gaelic. You want to prepare yourself before speaking to him by writing the order out in Gaelic first.

black tea with sugar
two coffees with milk
black coffee without sugar
tea without milk or sugar
two orange juices
white tea with sugar

tì dhubh le siùcar

dà chofaidh le bainne, cofaidh dubh gun siùcar, tì gun bhainne is gun siùcar, dà shùgh orains, tì gheal le siùcar

ASKING SOMEONE WHAT THEY WHAT

To ask someone what they want, you say

dè tha sibh ag iarraidh? (*jay ha shiv uh gee-uhree*)
– what do you want?

To a close friend or a child, use
dè tha thu ag iarraidh? – what do you want?

SAYING WHAT YOU WANT

tha mi ag iarraidh... (*ha me uh gee-uhree*) –
I want...

tha mi ag iarraidh cupa cofaidh – I want a cup
of coffee

tha mi ag iarraidh còc (*kohk*) – I want a coke

Taigh-Osda Eilean a' Cheò
Misty Isle Hotel
Licensed

còc – coke

sùgh orains

fìon gun alcol (*feeuhn guhn ahlkohl*) –
non-alcoholic wine

fìon geal – white wine

fìon dearg (*jehrahk*) – red wine

pinnt (*peehntch*) – pint

leth-phinnt (*lyayh-feehntch*) – half a pint

làgar (*laahguhr*) – lager

leann (*lyewhn*) – beer

uisge-beatha (*ushkuh-behuh*) – whisky

branndaidh (*brahwndee*) – brandy

bhodca (*vawdkah*) – vodka

ORDERING IN QUANTITIES

pinnt leann (*peehntch lyewhn*) – a pint of beer

leth-phinnt làgair (*lyayh-feehntch laahguhyr*) –
half a pint of lager

dà phinnt (*daa feehntch*) – two pints

glainne fìon (*glahnyuh feeuhn*) – a glass of wine

dà ghlainne còc (*daa ghlahnyuh kohk*) –
two glasses of coke

The following are very common too:

drama (*drahmuh*) – a dram

and

tè bheag (*chayh vayhk*) – a small one
(a single measure of spirits)

Think of the name of this whisky,
which is from Gaelic.

SAYING IT'S A PLEASURE

The following phrase can be used when someone thanks
you for something:

's e ur beatha (*sheh uhr behuh*) – it's a pleasure

The less formal form is

's e do bheatha (*sheh doh vehuh*) - it's a pleasure

Ag iarraidh deoch
Asking for drinks

ORDERING IN THE BAR

A large coach party has just arrived for refreshments, and you have been asked to help with the bar orders. Use the checklist to keep a count of each order.

Tha mi ag iarraidh fìon dearg.

Dà phinnt leann.

Tha mi ag iarraidh pinnt làgair.

Fìon geal.

Tha mi ag iarraidh glainne fìon gun alcol.

Glainne còc.

Tha mi ag iarraidh uisge-beatha.

Bhodca is còc, sùgh orains, agus leth-phinnt làgair.

A glass of coke	☐
A glass of non-alcoholic wine	☐
A glass of red wine	☐
A glass of white wine	☐
A half-pint of lager	☐
A pint of lager	☐
A vodka and coke	☐
A whisky	☐
An orange juice	☐
Two pints of beer	☐

CHEERS

To say cheers or good health, people say

slàinte mhath! *(slahnchuh vah)* – good health!

or just **slàinte!** on its own

[You may also hear **slàinte mhòr** *(slahnchuh vore)*, with the same meaning.]

WATER OF LIFE

The word whisky comes from the Gaelic word **uisge-beatha** which literally means 'water of life'. As some people say, you shouldn't put water in your whisky because there's already water in it!

MAKING UP AN ORDER

Link up words from each of the columns below to make up an order

cupa	làgair	....
sùgh	fìon	....
glainne	tì	....
cofaidh	còc	....
dà chupa	orains	....
tè	dubh	....
dà phinnt	cofaidh	....
glainne	bheag	....

cupa tì, sùgh orains, glainne fìon, cofaidh dubh, dà chupa cofaidh, tè bheag, dà phinnt làgair, glainne còc

Expressing an opinion
A' toirt seachad beachd

SAYING THAT YOU LIKE SOMETHING

is toigh leam... *(iss tuh lehwm)* – I like...

Some dialects use

is caomh leam... *(iss kaohv lehwm)* – I like...

SAYING THAT YOU DON'T LIKE SOMETHING

cha toigh leam... *(chah tuh lehwm)* – I don't like...

or

cha chaomh leam... *(chah chaohv lehwm)* – I don't like...

...idir *(eetchuhr)* – at all

is beag orm... *(iss bayhk awhrahm)* – I don't care for... or I hate...

TV PREFERENCES

A large TV company has asked you to help in conducting a survey of viewers' preferences. Read the following statements and tick off on the survey form which programmes people like and which they don't.

> Is toigh leam Haggis Agus.

> Is beag orm Donnie Murdo.

> Is toigh leam Machair.

Dè tha seo? (a game show)

> Cha toigh leam Seall.

Machair (a Gaelic soap opera)

> Is toigh leam Seall.

> Is toigh leam Donnie Murdo.

> Is caomh leam Dè tha seo?

> Cha toigh leam Haggis Agus.

Haggis Agus (a cookery programme)

> Cha toigh leam Machair idir.

Donnie Murdo (the Gaelic version of Danger Mouse)

> Cha toigh leam Dè tha seo? idir.

Seall (an environmental programme)

	Is toigh l' *(iss tuhl)*	Cha toigh l' *(chah tuhl)*
Haggis Agus	☐	☐
Machair	☐	☐
Seall	☐	☐
Donnie Murdo	☐	☐
Dè tha seo?	☐	☐

A
STEP BY STEP
CEUM AIR CHEUM

TALKING ABOUT YOUR INTERESTS

Taking each one of these pastimes in turn, say whether you like, don't like, or even hate it.

For example,

Is toigh leam
Cha toigh leam } golf
Is beag orm

coimhead air an telebhisean
(kohyuht ayhr uhn television) –
watching (the) television

....

....

golf *(golf)* – golf

....

....

leughadh *(lyayugh)* – reading

....

....

....

rugbaidh *(rugby)* – rugby

....

....

ball-coise *(bahwl koshuh)* – football

....

....

ruith *(ruiy)* – running

....

....

ceòl *(kyewhl)* – music

....

....

iomain *(eemehyn)* – shinty

....

....

....

seinn *(shuhyn)* – singing

....

....

....

gàirnealaireachd
(gaahrnehlehruchk) –
gardening

....

....

còcaireachd
(kawhkehruchk) – cooking

....

....

coiseachd *(koshuchk)* – walking

....

....

iasgach *(eeuskuch)* – fishing

....

....

snàmh *(snaahv)* – swimming

....

....

This page is linked to • TV Programme 6 • Audio Cassette 1

ASKING WHETHER SOMEONE LIKES SOMETHING

an toigh leibh...? *(uhn tuhl leeve)* – do you like...?

or

an caomh leibh...? *(uhn kaohv leeve)* – do you like..?

The form you will need when talking to a friend or to a child is

an toigh leat...? *(uhn tuhl leht)* – do you like...?

or

an caomh leat...? *(uhn kaohv leht)* – do you like...?

GIVING YOUR REPLY

To answer the question **an toigh leibh...?** – do you like...?, you will need

is toigh l' *(iss tuhl)* – yes, I like...

is toigh leam... – I like...

or

is caomh l' *(iss kaohl)* – yes, I like...

is caomh leam... *(iss kaohv lehwm)* – I like...

Notice how the **l** of **leam** is still pronounced when saying **is toigh** or **is caomh**.

FINDING OUT WHAT PEOPLE LIKE

You are on a marketing course and have been asked to compile a list of people's leisure pursuits. Ask each of these people whether they like what it is they are involved in, and complete their answers for them. Use the form **an toigh leat...?** when talking to anyone younger than you.

Expressing an opinion
A' toirt seachad beachd

A
STEP BY STEP
CEUM AIR CHEUM

SAYING WHETHER SOMETHING IS GOOD OR BAD

tha... – is... or are...

chan eil... – is not... or are not...

...math – ...good

...glè mhath – ...very good

...sgoinneil (*skuhnyehl*) – ... great, or brilliant

...glan (*glahn*) – ...great, or brilliant

...meadhanach math (*meeahnuch mah*) – ...fairly good

...dona –...bad

...grod (*grawht*) –...rotten, or rubbish

and these will be useful

seo – this

sin (*shin*) – that

JUDGING THE SHOW

You have been asked to judge the baking entries at the local show. Give each entry a mark out of ten (**a-mach à deich**), and write an appropriate comment against each.

Mark _Còig_

Comment _Tha seo meadhanach math._

This page is linked to • TV Programme 6 • Audio Cassette 1

SAYING WHETHER YOU ENJOYED SOMETHING

chòrd ... rium *(chawhrst ... rewhm)* – I enjoyed…

chòrd sin rium – I enjoyed that

(Literally, that pleased me.)

ASKING SOMEONE WHETHER THEY ENJOYED SOMETHING

an do chòrd ... ruibh? *(uhn duh chawhrst ... ruhyv)* – did you enjoy…?

an do chòrd sin ruibh? – did you enjoy that?

or, to a friend or a child, you would use

an do chòrd ... riut? *(uhn duh chawhrst ... rewht)* – did you enjoy…?

To reply, use

chòrd, chòrd ... rium – yes, I enjoyed…

or

cha do chòrd, cha do chòrd ... rium *(chah duh chawhrst)* – no, I didn't enjoy...

HOW DID YOU ENJOY THE MEAL?

You have been asked to comment on your meal in a restaurant. Say whether you did or didn't enjoy the various items.

an sùgh orains

an sùgh tomàto *(uhn sooh tomato)*

an t-iasg *(uhn cheeusk)*

an fheòil *(uhn ehywl)*

a' ghlasraich *(uh ghlasreech)*

am brot *(uhm brawht)*

am mìlsean *(uhm meehlshuhn)*

an cofaidh

An do chòrd ... ruibh?	
an sùgh orains:	Cha do chòrd.
an sùgh tomàto:	Chòrd.
am brot:	....
an t-iasg:	....
an fheòil:	....
a' ghlasraich:	....
am mìlsean:	....
an cofaidh:	....

Discussing children
A' bruidhinn mu chloinn

STEP BY STEP
CEUM AIR CHEUM

ASKING SOMEONE WHETHER THEY HAVE CHILDREN

a bheil clann agaibh? *(uh vayhl klahwn ackuhv)* – do you have children?

It's also common for people to ask whether you have a family:

a bheil teaghlach agaibh?
(uh vayhl chyuhluch ackuhv) – do you have a family?

To reply, if you have, you say

tha – yes, I do

and if you haven't, you say

chan eil – no, I don't

or

chan eil fhathast – not yet

The word **clann** can also mean descendants and from it we get the English word clan.

SONS AND DAUGHTERS

mac – a son

nighean *(nyeeuhn)* – a daughter

leanabh *(lyehnuhv)* – a baby

pàisde *(paashchuh)* – a child

(The word **clann** is singular but always has a plural meaning.)

GIRLS AND BOYS

Different dialects use different sets of words for girl and boy. You'll be understood, though, whichever you use.

balach *(bahluch)* – a boy
or
gille *(geehluh)* – a boy

caileag *(kahlahk)* – a girl
or
nighean – a girl

(Notice that **nighean** can mean a girl or a daughter.)

The English word gillie or ghillie comes from the Gaelic word **gille**, though now it means someone who helps in fishing or hunting.

WORD GAME

Find the following words in the grid:

clann **teaghlach** **mac** **nighean**
balach **caileag** **gille**

T	E	B	C	H	C	L	A	L	N	N	T	A
C	B	B	A	L	A	C	H	T	A	N	E	A
A	C	L	D	C	A	N	L	C	M	M	A	T
I	L	A	G	A	A	N	A	B	A	H	G	G
L	A	C	F	E	L	I	N	A	A	G	H	E
E	N	N	H	M	A	C	L	A	N	U	L	R
I	I	G	L	A	B	I	S	E	A	M	A	G
B	I	E	L	L	I	G	S	G	A	H	C	I
N	F	S	A	M	P	O	E	L	I	G	H	L

(Words can be read in any direction.)

Discussing children
A' bruidhinn mu chloinn

COUNTING HEADS

When talking about people, you generally use a special set of numbers from two to ten.

2	**dithis**	*(jeeish)*
3	**triùir**	*(trewhr)*
4	**ceathrar**	*(kehruhr)*
5	**còignear**	*(kohyknuhr)*
6	**sianar**	*(sheeahnuhr)*
7	**seachdnar**	*(shehchknuhr)*
8	**ochdnar**	*(awchknuhr)*
9	**naoinear**	*(nuhynuhr)*
10	**deichnear**	*(juhychnuhr)*

These numbers may change the initial sound of a following word. For example, **balach** becomes **bhalach**

dithis bhalach *(jeeish vahluch)* – two boys

triùir chaileag *(trewhr chahlahk)* – three girls

ceathrar mhac *(kehruhr vachk)* – four sons

còignear chloinne *(kohyknuhr chluhnyuh)* – five children

sianar ghillean *(sheeahnuhr yeebluhn)* – six boys

The word **nighean** doesn't change its spelling though the sound of the n can change slightly.

seachdnar nighean *(shehchknuhr neeuhn)* – seven girls

A
STEP BY STEP
CEUM AIR CHEUM

COUNTING THE CHILDREN

While on holiday, you ask a number of people you meet whether they have any children. They all say **tha**, yes, but then they add how many boys or how many girls they have. They all use the words **balach** and **nighean**.

From these pictures, write out their answers. The first one is completed for you. The other answers are given at the foot of the page.

A bheil clann agaibh?

Tha. Triùir bhalach agus nighean.

....

....

....

....

....

....

2. Tha. Dithis bhalach.
3. Tha. Triùir bhalach.
4. Tha. Dithis bhalach.
5. Tha. Ceathrar nighean.
6. Tha. Dithis nighean.
7. Tha. Dithis nighean agus balach.

Discussing children
A' bruidhinn mu chloinn

SAYING THAT YOU HAVE CHILDREN

tha … agam – I have …

tha balach agus nighean agam – I have a boy and a girl

tha … againn (ackeeyn) – we have …

tha dithis nighean agus dithis bhalach againn – we have two girls and two boys

SAYING THAT YOU DON'T HAVE CHILDREN

chan eil … agam – I don't have …

chan eil clann agam – I don't have any children

chan eil … againn – we don't have…

FITTING THEM ALL IN!

You are organizing your local charity run for the children's annual outing. Each of these drivers is saying how many children he is carrying. Keep a count of the numbers – there should be twenty-one altogether!

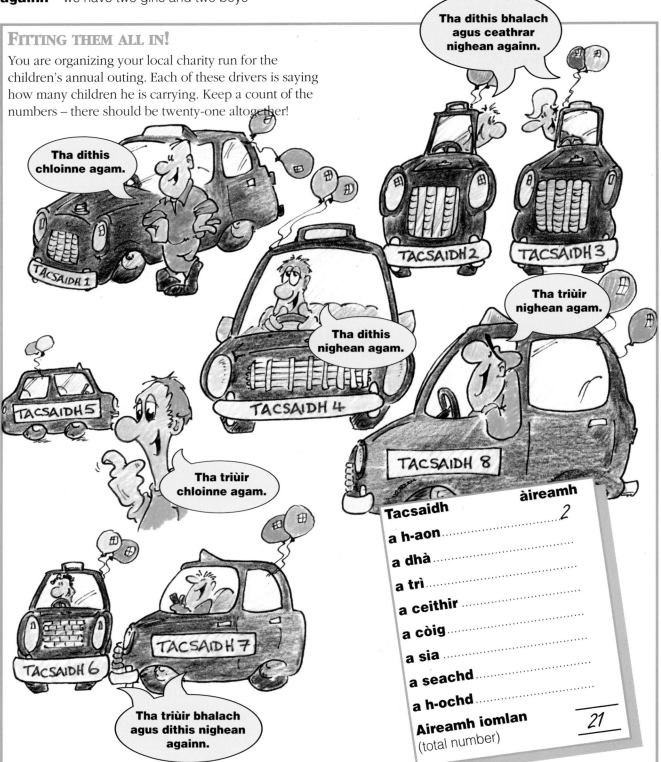

Tha dithis bhalach agus ceathrar nighean againn.

Tha dithis chloinne agam.

Tha dithis nighean agam.

Tha triùir nighean agam.

Tha triùir chloinne agam.

Tha triùir bhalach agus dithis nighean againn.

Tacsaidh	àireamh
	2
a h-aon	
a dhà	
a trì	
a ceithir	
a còig	
a sia	
a seachd	
a h-ochd	
Aireamh iomlan (total number)	21

This page is linked to • TV Programme 7 • Audio Cassette 2

INTRODUCING YOUR CHILDREN

seo... – this is... (followed by the name)

seo...

...am mac agam – ...my son

...an nighean agam – ...my daughter, or my girl

...a' chaileag agam – ...my girl

...am balach agam – ...my boy

...an gille agam – ...my boy

seo a' chlann agam *(chlahwn)* – these are my children

SORTING THE CENSUS FIGURES

Information about the number of Gaelic speaking children from different houses in a Highland village has been partly destroyed because of computer failure. Use the English version to link the numbers with the correct words.

2 children
3 boys
4 girls
3 children
3 girls
2 sons
4 children
2 boys

dithis bhalach ceathrar chloinne triùir mhac dithis nighean dithis chloinne ceathrar nighean triùir bhalach triùir chloinne

....

....

....

....

....

....

....

....

TALKING WITH PARENTS

You are attending a Saturday club with your children, and meet up with some of the other parents over a cuppa. Read through the following dialogue, and then take the part of B, answering questions according to your own situation.

A. **Hallò! Madainn mhath.**

B. **Madainn mhath.**

A. **Ciamar a tha sibh?**

B. **Tha gu math, tapadh leibh. Ciamar a tha sibh fèin?**

A. **Chan eil dona. A bheil sibh ag iarraidh cupa tì?**

B. **Tha. Tapadh leibh.**

A. **A bheil clann agaibh?**

B. **Tha. Tha triùir agam. Tha balach agus dithis nighean agam. A bheil clann agaibh fèin?**

A. **Tha. Tha nighean agus dithis bhalach agam............A! Seo Seonag, an nighean agam.**
(to Seonag) **Ciamar a tha thu?**

Seonag: **Tha gu math, tapadh leibh.**

A. **Dè tha thu ag iarraidh?**

Seonag: **Tha mi ag iarraidh sùgh orains, mas e ur toil e!**

A. **Glè mhath.** (Seonag runs off)
Càit a bheil sibh a' fuireach?

B. **Tha mi a' fuireach anns a' bhaile. Càit a bheil sibh fèin a' fuireach?**

A. **O! Tha mi a' fuireach air Sràid a' Bhanca....**

A. Hello! Good morning.
B. Good morning.
A. How are you?
B. Fine, thanks. How are you?
A. Not bad. Do you want a cup of tea?
B. Yes. Thank you.
A. Do you have any children?
B. Yes. I've got three. I've got a boy and two girls. Do you have any children?
A. Yes. I've got a girl and two boys. Ah! This is Seonag, my daughter.
(to Seonag) How are you?
Seonag: Fine, thanks.
A. What do you want?
Seonag: I want some orange juice, please.
A. Very well. (Seonag runs off)
Where do you live?
B. I live in town. Where do you live?
A. Oh! I live on Bank Street...

ASKING SOMEONE THE TIME

dè an uair a tha e? *(jay uhn oouhyr uh ha eh)* – what time is it?

TELLING THE TIME BY THE HOUR

To say one o'clock, you say

uair – one o'clock

(**Uair** also means an hour)

For two o'clock, you say

dà uair – two o'clock

To say three o'clock up to ten o'clock, you use the plural form **uairean** for hours

trì uairean *(tree oouhyruhn)* – three o'clock

deich uairean – ten o'clock

Eleven o'clock and twelve o'clock are 'one hour teen' and 'two hour teen'

aon uair deug *(aohn oouhyr jeeuhk)* – eleven o'clock

dà uair dheug *(daa oouhyr yeeuk)* – twelve o'clock

There is also a shortened form of twelve o'clock, **dà reug** *(daa rake)*

AT THE STROKE OF

To say at one o'clock, at two o'clock, and so on, use

aig *(eck)* – at

aig uair – at one o'clock

aig dà uair – at two o'clock

SAYING WHAT TIME IT IS

tha e ... – it is …

tha e trì uairean – it's three o'clock

tha e aon uair deug – it's eleven o'clock

THE EFFECT OF 2

We have already seen how the word **dà** can affect the letters at the beginning of words, for example **dà chofaidh, dà fhichead**.

A vowel cannot be followed by h, so two o'clock is just **dà uair.**

In the phrase for twelve o'clock, however, the beginning of **deug** is affected: **dà uair dheug**.

dà uair dheug

aon uair deug

uair

deich uairean

dà uair

naoi uairean

trì uairean

ochd uairean

ceithir uairean

seachd uairean

còig uairean

sia uairean

Telling the time
Ag innse na h-uarach

MAKING APPOINTMENTS

Here are the times for a number of appointments and meetings which you have to arrange over the phone.

Write the times out in words to prepare you for saying them.

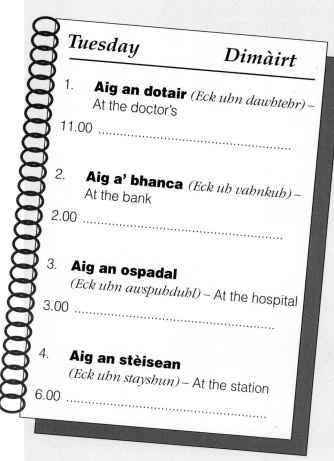

Tuesday   *Dimàirt*

1. **Aig an dotair** *(Eck uhn dawhtehr)* –
At the doctor's
11.00 ....

2. **Aig a' bhanca** *(Eck uh vahnkuh)* –
At the bank
2.00 ....

3. **Aig an ospadal**
(Eck uhn awspuhduhl) – At the hospital
3.00 ....

4. **Aig an stèisean**
(Eck uhn stayshun) – At the station
6.00 ....

ROUGHLY ON TIME

gu bhith... *(goob veeh)* – nearly...

tha e gu bhith uair *(ha eh gooh veeh oouhyr)* –
it's nearly one o'clock

timcheall air... *(cheemeechuhl ayhr)* – about...

tha e timcheall air ceithir uairean –
it's about four o'clock

BEING MORE PRECISE

cairteal an dèidh *(kahrstyahl uhn jay)* –
quarter past...

leth-uair an dèidh *(lyayh-oouhyr uhn jay)* –
half past...

cairteal gu *(kahrstyahl gooh)* – quarter to...

CATCHING THE BOAT

Caledonian MacBrayne
Hebridean and Clyde Ferries

AISEAG SGALPAIGH

8.45 agus...

There will be extra sailings on the Scalpay ferry today, and a new timetable has to be written up on the board.

These were the revised times given over the phone by the ferryman. Jot the various times down in figures.

**Aig cairteal gu naoi
agus cairteal an dèidh naoi.**

**Aig leth-uair an dèidh aon uair deug
agus cairteal an dèidh dà uair dheug.**

**Aig cairteal gu trì
agus leth-uair an dèidh còig.**

Telling the time
Ag innse na h-uarach

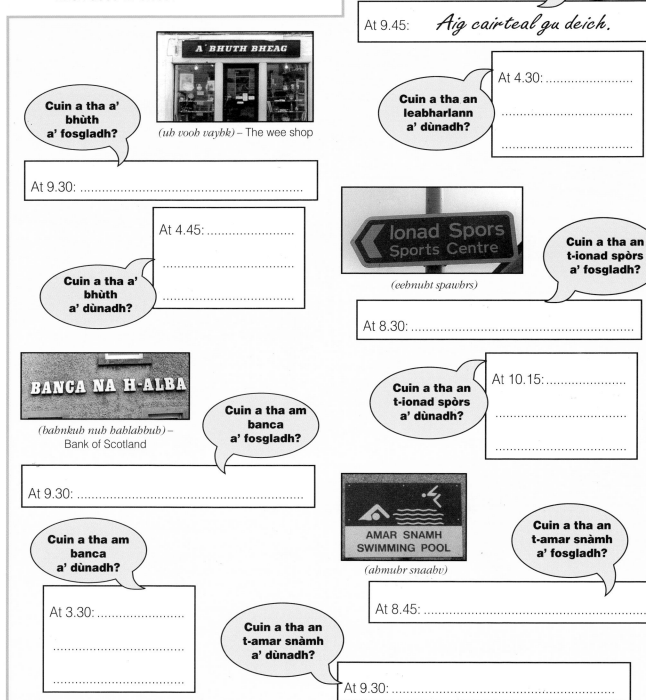

ASKING ABOUT OPENING AND CLOSING TIMES

To ask when something opens, you say

cuin a tha ... a' fosgladh?

> *(koohyn uh ha ... uh fawhsklugh)* –
> when does ... open?

And to ask when something closes, you say

cuin a tha ... a' dùnadh?

> *(koohyn uh ha ... uh doohnugh)* –
> when does ... close?

HELPING OUT WITH TIMES

You are asked questions about the opening and closing times of services in the area. Write out the answers as you would say them.

Leabharlann Library

(lyewhuhrlahwn)

Cuin a tha an leabharlann a' fosgladh?

At 9.45: *Aig cairteal gu deich.*

Cuin a tha an leabharlann a' dùnadh?

At 4.30: ....

....

....

A' BHUTH BHEAG

(uh vooh vayhk) – The wee shop

Cuin a tha a' bhùth a' fosgladh?

At 9.30: ....

Cuin a tha a' bhùth a' dùnadh?

At 4.45: ....

....

....

BANCA NA H-ALBA

(bahnkuh nuh hahlahbuh) –
Bank of Scotland

Cuin a tha am banca a' fosgladh?

At 9.30: ....

Cuin a tha am banca a' dùnadh?

At 3.30: ....

....

....

Ionad Spors Sports Centre

(eehnuht spawhrs)

Cuin a tha an t-ionad spòrs a' fosgladh?

At 8.30: ....

Cuin a tha an t-ionad spòrs a' dùnadh?

At 10.15: ....

....

....

AMAR SNAMH SWIMMING POOL

(ahmuhr snaahv)

Cuin a tha an t-amar snàmh a' fosgladh?

At 8.45: ....

Cuin a tha an t-amar snàmh a' dùnadh?

At 9.30: ....

ASKING ABOUT TRAVELLING TIMES

The following will be useful

cuin a tha ... a' falbh?
> *(koohyn uh ha ... uh fahlahv)* –
> when does ... leave?

cuin a tha ... a' ruighinn
> *(... uh ruyheeyn)* –
> when does...arrive

am bus *(uhm buhs)* – the bus

an trèan *(uhn treyhn)* – the train

am plèan *(uhm pleyhn)* – the plane

am bàta *(uhm baahtuh)* – the boat

TELL THE TIME

Work out the times on the following clocks and jot them down in the spaces provided.

Then, turn the page on its side and start again. Two more turns of the page will give you plenty of practice.

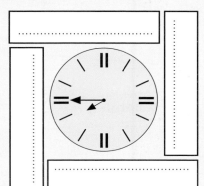

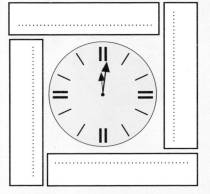

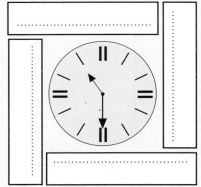

DEPARTURE AND ARRIVAL TIMES

Take the part of the assistant at the information desk below. The pattern for the answer is the same every time.

tha am bus a' falbh aig... – the bus leaves at...

tha an trèan a' ruighinn aig... – the train arrives at...

RUIGHINN		
à (from) Dùn Eideann	8.45
Sruighlea	9.00
Port Rìgh	9.15
FALBH		
gu (to) Dùn Eideann	9.30
Sruighlea	10.15
Port Rìgh	11.00

RUIGHINN		
à (from) Inbhir Nis	8.30
Dùn Dèagh	11.00
Glaschu	12.00
FALBH		
gu (to) Inbhir Nis	10.00
Dùn Dèagh	1.00
Glaschu	2.00

Cuin a tha an trèan à Inbhir Nis a' ruighinn?

Cuin a tha an trèan gu Dùn Dèagh a' falbh?

Cuin a tha an trèan à Glaschu a' ruighinn?

Cuin a tha am bus gu Dùn Eideann a' falbh?

Cuin a tha am bus gu Port Rìgh a' falbh?

Discussing jobs
A' bruidhinn mu obraichean

SAYING WHAT JOB YOU DO

's e ... a th' annam *(sheh ... uh hahnuhm)* – I'm a...

AT THE JOB CENTRE

A friend of yours is looking for a change of job.
Perhaps one of the following would be of interest.
You can guess the meaning of some Gaelic words for
occupations as they are similar in many languages.
What jobs are people saying they do here?
The answers are given below.

1. **'S e tidsear a th' annam** *(teechuhr)*

2. **'S e nurs a th' annam** *(nurse)*

3. **'S e dràibhear a th' annam** *(drivuhr)*

4. **'S e portair a th' annam** *(pawrstehr)*

5. **'S e còcaire a th' annam** *(kawhkihruh)*

6. **'S e dotair a th' annam** *(dawhtehr)*

7. **'S e ministear a th' annam** *(meenishchehr)*

8. **'S e poileas a th' annam** *(pawhluhs)*

9. **'S e posta a th' annam** *(pawstuh)*

10. **'S e bancair a th' annam** *(bahnkehr)*

11. **'S e bèicear a th' annam** *(behkehr)*

12. **'S e bùidsear a th' annam** *(boohchehr)*

USING PEOPLE'S WORK TITLES

Some people are often referred to by using their job title
along with their name.

an Dotair MacLeòid – Doctor Macleod
(literally, the Doctor Macleod)

an t-Urramach MacNèill *(uhn toohruhmuch)* –
Reverend MacNeil.

a' Bhànrigh Ealasaid *(uh vahwnree Ehlihsetch)*
– Queen Elizabeth

am Prionnsa Teàrlach *(uhm prewhsuh Chehrluch)*
– Prince Charles

1. teacher. 2. nurse. 3. driver. 4. porter. 5. cook. 6. doctor. 7. minister.
8. police officer. 9. postman. 10. banker. 11. baker. 12. butcher.

This page is linked to • **TV Programme 9** • **Audio Cassette 2**

A STEP BY STEP CEUM AIR CHEUM

KNOW YOUR NEIGHBOUR

Following the example, take each neighbour's part in turn and introduce yourself.

Iain – saor

Is mise Iain. 'S e saor a th' annam.

Eilidh – clèireach

Seònaid – bean-taighe

Ailean – peantair

Mòrag - reiceadair

Dòmhnall – tuathanach

Anna – cunntasair

Uisdean – clachair

saor *(suhr)* – carpenter
clèireach *(klayhruch)* – clerk
bean-taighe *(behn tehuh)* – housewife
peantair *(pehntehr)* – painter
tuathanach *(tooubahnuch)* – farmer
cunntasair *(koohntuhsehr)* – accountant
clachair *(klachehr)* – bricklayer
reiceadair *(ruhykuhdehr)* – salesperson

Discussing jobs
A' bruidhinn mu obraichean

A STEP BY STEP CEUM AIR CHEUM

SAYING WHERE YOU WORK

tha mi ag obair… *(uh gohpuhr)* – I work…

…ann an oifis *(awhfeesh)* – …in an office

…ann an ospadal *(awhspuhduhl)* – …in a hospital

…ann an sgoil *(sgawl)* – …in a school

…ann an stèisean *(stayshun)* – …in a station

…ann an cafaidh *(kahfee)* – …in a café

(Notice that **ann an** becomes **ann am** before words beginning in b –)

…ann am banca *(bahnkuh)* – in a bank

…ann am bùth *(booh)* – in a shop

and

…aig an taigh *(tuyh)* – …at home

…air tuathanas *(toouhahnuhs)* – on a farm

…air croit *(krawhch)* – on a croft

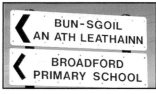

ASKING WHERE SOMEONE WORKS

càit a bheil sibh ag obair? – where do you work?

Remember, if you're talking to a close friend, use **thu**

càit a bheil thu ag obair? – where do you work?

PLACING WHERE SOMEONE WORKS

You've just joined a local group, and the subject of jobs turns up. A number of people tell you what they do for a living. Put yourself in their position and say where you work.

'S e tidsear a th' annam. Tha mi ag obair ann an sgoil.

'S e clèireach a th' annam.
....

'S e nurs a th' annam.
....

'S e portair a th' annam.
....

'S e tuathanach a th' annam.
....

'S e còcaire a th' annam.
....

'S e reiceadair a th' annam.
....

'S e bancair a th' annam.
....

'S e cunntasair a th' annam.
....

Discussing jobs
A' bruidhinn mu obraichean

SAYING WHO YOU WORK FOR

To say you work for a person or company, you use **aig**

tha mi ag obair aig... – I work for…

Tha mi ag obair aig Eisd.

To say you work for yourself, you use

...air mo cheann fhìn (*ayhr mohw chehwn heehn*) – …for myself

tha mi ag obair air mo cheann fhìn – I work for myself

SAYING THAT YOU'RE NOT WORKING

chan eil mi ag obair – I'm not working

...an-dràsda (*uhn draahstuh*) – …just now

tha mi gun obair (*ha me guhn ohpuhr*) – I'm out of work, or I'm unemployed

tha mi air m' obair a leigeil dhìom
(*ha me ayhr mohpuhr uh leehkehl yeeuhm*) – I've retired

ASKING PEOPLE ABOUT THEIR JOBS

dè an obair a th' agaibh?
(*jay uhn ohpuhr uh hackuhv*) – what's your job?, or what job do you have?

and

càit a bheil sibh ag obair...? – where do you work…?

...an-dràsda – …just now

Remember that to a close friend you would use **agad** instead of **agaibh**, and **thu** instead of **sibh**

dè an obair a th' agad? – what's your job?

càit a bheil thu ag obair? – where do you work?

Càit a bheil sibh ag obair an-dràsda?

Tha mi ag obair aig Banca na h-Alba.

Dè an obair a th' agad an-dràsda?

O! Tha mi ag obair ann an taigh-òsda. 'S e còcaire a th' annam.

Tha mi ag obair ann am bùth.

Càit a bheil thu ag obair an-dràsda?

IDENTIKITS

Choose one of the pictures. Then answer the questions in the middle of the page. Read them aloud, or get another player to do so. You'll find clues to the correct answers in your picture.

1. **Ciamar a tha sibh?**
2. **Dè an t-ainm a th' oirbh?**
3. **Càit a bheil sibh a' fuireach?**
4. **Dè an seòladh a th' agaibh?**
5. **Dè an àireamh fòn a th' agaibh?**
6. **Cò às a tha sibh?**
7. **An toigh leibh ball-coise?**
   An toigh leibh snàmh?
   An toigh leibh iasgach?
   An toigh leibh còcaireachd?
8. **A bheil clann agaibh?**
9. **Dè an obair a th' agaibh?**

Saying hello
Ag ràdh hallò

Gaelic can be part of your everyday routine from the start. Use these simple phrases to greet your child and family in the morning and to say good night.

hallò, a ghràidh *(uh ghraay)* – hello, dear

madainn mhath, a ghràidh – good morning, dear

oidhche mhath, a ghràidh *(uhychuh)* – good night, dear

Instead of **a ghràidh**, some people use **a ghaoil** *(uh ghuhyl)*.

SAYING THANK YOU

tapadh leat *(tahpuh leht)* – thank you

[Instead of **tapadh leat, tapadh leibh** is generally used towards older people, or people you do not know well. There is more about this in the *Ceum air Cheum* section.]

PRAISING YOUR CHILD

glè mhath, a ghràidh – very good, dear

tha sin math – that's good

athair *(ahhehr)* – father, **Dadaidh** – daddy
madainn mhath – good morning
a' phiseag *(uh feeshahk)* – the kitten, **an cuilean** *(uhn koolahn)* – the puppy

oidhche mhath, a Mhamaidh – good night, Mummy
Mamaidh – Mummy, **màthair** *(mah-hehr)* – mother
doras *(dawhruhs)* – a door, **leabaidh** *(lyepeeh)* – a bed

Ag ràdh hallò

THE BEGINNING OF THE SCHOOL DAY

Here parents and children, and the teacher, are saying hello or goodbye to each other:

ciamar a tha thu? – how are you?

The more formal version for greeting adults is:
ciamar a tha sibh? – how are you?

tìoraidh *(cheerie)* – cheerio

Did you notice the girl saying **tìoraidh** to her mother?

uinneag *(uhnyahk)* – a window, **am bòrd** *(uhm bawrst)* – the table
an sèithear *(uhn shayhuhr)* – the chair, **an tidsear** *(uhn teechahr)* – the teacher
Calum, am balach – Calum, the boy, **dèideagan** *(jaydyahkuhn)* – toys
Màiri, an nighean – Mary, the girl, **màthair Màiri** – Mary's mother

FALACH-FEAD

càit a bheil thu? – where are you?

sin thu! – there you are!

Talking about times of the day and the weather
A' bruidhinn mu amannan san latha is mun t-sìde

tha an t-àm agad ... – it's time for you ...

... **èirigh** *(ayreeh)* – ... to get up

... **ithe** *(eechuh)* – ... to eat

... **a dhol a-mach**
(uh dhol uh mach) –
... to go out

... **cluich(e)** *(cluych[uh])* – ... to play

... **a dhol dhan leabaidh** *(uh dhol dhan lyepeeh)*
– ... to go to bed

DISCUSSING THE WEATHER

tha latha math ann *(ha lahuh mah ahwn)*
– it's a nice day

tha an sneachd ann *(ha uhn shnyehck ahwn)*
– it's snowing

tha an t-uisge ann *(ha uhn tushkuh ahwn)*
– it's raining

GETTING YOUR CHILD'S ATTENTION

trobhad *(trohuht)* – come (here)

seall *(shawhl)* – look

tiugainn *(tyukeen)* – let's go

greas ort *(grayhs awhrst)* – hurry up

siuthad *(shoo-uht)* – go on

HELPING YOUR CHILD TO COLOUR A PICTURE
Help your child to colour this picture using the colour code.

dubh   **geal**

donn (dowhn)   **gorm** (gawhruhm)   **dearg** (dyeyruhg)   **uaine** (ooahnyuh)   **buidhe** (booyuh)

What sort of day is it? ....

tha a' bhracaist deiseil *(ha uh vrehckusht dyehschehl)*
– breakfast is ready

tha an diathad deiseil *(dyeeuhuht)* – lunch is ready

tha an dìnnear deiseil *(dyeenyuhr)* – dinner is ready

a bheil thu ag iarraidh... ? – do you want... ?

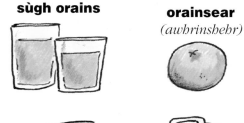

sùgh orains

orainsear
(awhrinshehr)

ubhal
(ooahl)

banana

ugh
(ooh)

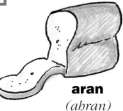

aran
(ahran)

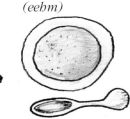

ìm
(eehm)

cofaidh

tì

siùcar

tost
(tawst)

lite
(lyeechuh)

bainne

isbeanan
(eeshbahnuhn)

càise
(cahshuh)

feòil
(fehywl)

buntàta
(buntahtuh)

brot

silidh
(sheeleeh)

slisneagan
(shleeshnyahguhn)

iasg

brisgean
(breeshkuhn)

rolaichean
(rawhleechuhn)

ith do bhiadh! *(eech doh veeugh)* – eat up! (eat your food)

TABLE MANNERS

mas e ur toil e – please

this is used by children to adults

tha, mas e ur toil e – yes, please

chan eil, tapadh leibh – no, thanks

mas e do thoil e – please

this is used by adults to children

A' cunntais agus ag ainmeachadh badan dhen bhodhaig

THE BODY

A' bhodhaig
(uh voheek)

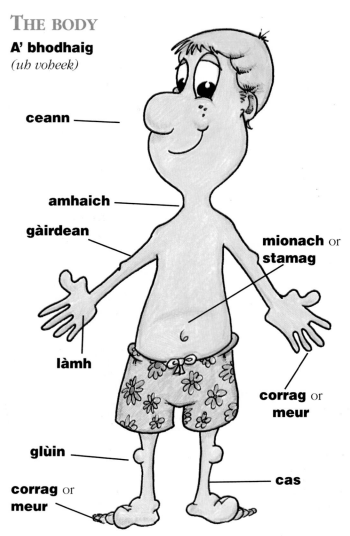

ceann

amhaich

gàirdean

mionach or stamag

làmh

corrag or meur

glùin

cas

corrag or meur

ceann – head, **amhaich** *(awheech)* – neck
gàirdean *(gaahrstehn)* – arm, **mionach** or **stamag** – tummy
làmh *(laahv)* – hand, **corrag** *(kawhrack)* or **meur** *(meeahr)* –
finger or toe, **glùin** *(glooohyn)* – knee, **cas** *(cass)* – leg or foot

THE HEAD

An ceann *(uhn cyawhn)*

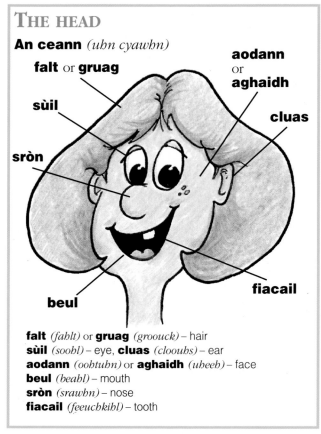

falt or gruag

aodann or aghaidh

sùil

cluas

sròn

fiacail

beul

falt *(fahlt)* or **gruag** *(groouck)* – hair
sùil *(soohl)* – eye, **cluas** *(cloouhs)* – ear
aodann *(oohtuhn)* or **aghaidh** *(uheeh)* – face
beul *(beahl)* – mouth
sròn *(srawhn)* – nose
fiacail *(feeuchkihl)* – tooth

NAMING THE FINGERS

Fingers in Gaelic have special names – though these are
most frequently used in a children's rhyme, which you'll
find on page 64.

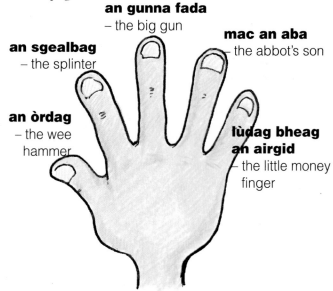

an gunna fada
– the big gun

mac an aba
– the abbot's son

an sgealbag
– the splinter

an òrdag
– the wee hammer

lùdag bheag
an airgid
– the little money finger

an òrdag *(uhn awhrdack)* – the thumb
an sgealbag *(uhn skehlahback)* – the index finger
an gunna fada *(uhn goohnuh fahduh)* – the third finger
mac an aba *(machk uhn ahbuh)* – the fourth finger
lùdag bheag an airgid – *(loohdack vayk uhn ehrickitch)* –
    the pinky

Some people use **calgag** *(kahlakahk)* or **eilbheag**
(ehluhvahk) instead of **sgealbag** for the index finger.

COUNTING WITH YOUR CHILD

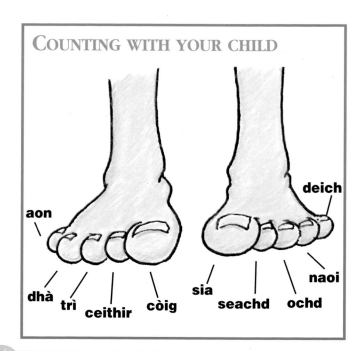

aon

deich

dhà

trì

ceithir

còig

sia

seachd

ochd

naoi

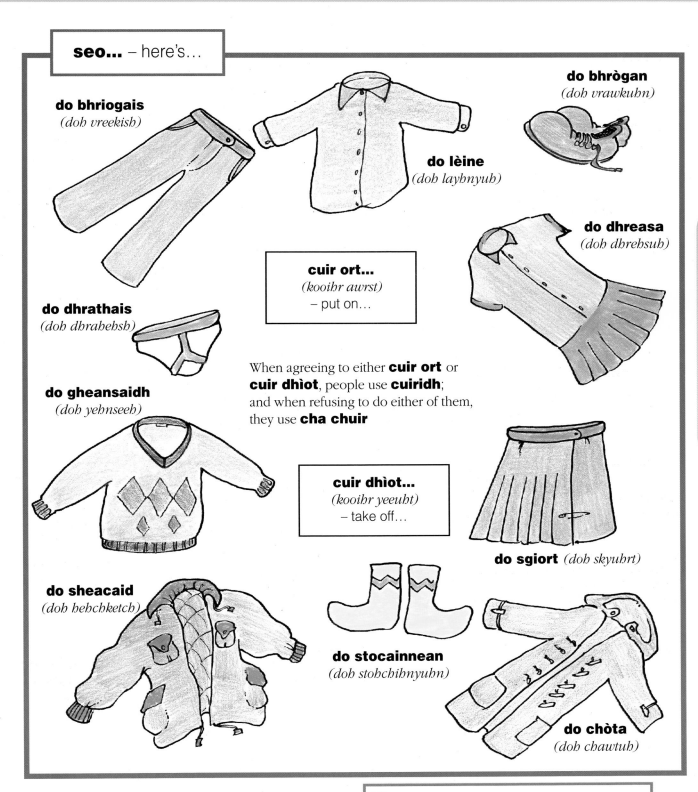

seo... – here's...

do bhriogais
(doh vreekish)

do lèine
(doh layhnyuh)

do bhrògan
(doh vrawkuhn)

do dhreasa
(doh dhrehsuh)

cuir ort...
(kooihr awrst)
– put on...

do dhrathais
(doh dhrahehsh)

When agreeing to either **cuir ort** or
cuir dhìot, people use **cuiridh**;
and when refusing to do either of them,
they use **cha chuir**

do gheansaidh
(doh yehnseeh)

cuir dhìot...
(kooihr yeeuht)
– take off...

do sgiort *(doh skyuhrt)*

do sheacaid
(doh hehchketch)

do stocainnean
(doh stohchihnyuhn)

do chòta
(doh chawtuh)

faigh... *(fieh)* – get or fetch...

faigh do sheacaid! *(fieh doh hehcketch)*
        – fetch your jacket!

THE POINTING GAME:

càit a bheil do ... ? – where's your ... ?

To answer, your child could point to the article
of clothing in the picture and say
an sin! – there!

The MacLeods have moved to Glasgow and Mrs MacLeod has gone to an estate agent to look for a new house

She goes in and sits down, where an estate agent greets her "Hello, how are you?"

Mrs MacLeod replies politely "Fine, thank you. How are you ?"

She asks for details of a house and is delighted with them "Very good!"

Mr MacLeod joins his wife. They say "Hello" and the estate agent offers Mr MacLeod a seat

The estate agent welcomes Mr MacLeod "Good afternoon. It's a fine day today!"

Mr MacLeod replies briefly "It is!"

He looks at the house details but is not impressed

The MacLeods arrive to see the new house but Mr. MacLeod hangs back

> Hallò! Dè an t-ainm a th' oirbh?

The estate agent meets Mrs MacLeod and the children "Hello! What's your name?"

> Mrs MacLeod. Seo Eilidh, an nighean agam.

Mrs MacLeod gives her name and then introduces Eilidh "Mrs MacLeod. This is Eilidh, my daughter."

> Agus seo Eòghann, am mac agam.

Then Mrs Macleod introduces Ewen "And this is Ewen, my son."

> Is mise Eilidh NicLeòid, agus seo Eòghann MacLeòid.

But Eilidh wants to introduce <u>herself</u> – and Ewen

> Is mise Mr Fleming. Thig a-steach!

The estate agent introduces himself to the children and invites them in

> Thig a-steach, Iain!

Mrs MacLeod looks round for her husband, who is still holding back "Come in, Iain!"

> Hallò, Mr MacLeod.

Mr Fleming welcomes Mr MacLeod into the house "Hello, Mr MacLeod."

MacLeod ... MacLeòid.

The MacLeods have bought the house and are busy settling in. Mr MacLeod repeats his name from the name-plate

They have renamed the house "My House"

Tigger!

While they are busy, their cat, Tigger, runs away

Ceart, ma-tha. Ainm?

Tigger.

The police have come to take details of Tigger's disappearance
"Right then. Name?"

Gabh mo leisgeul.

The policeman tries to hide his amusement
"Excuse me."

Dè an seòladh a th' agaibh?

Còig Rathad Strathpollock.

"What's your address?"
"Five Strathpollock Road."

Dè an àireamh fòn a th' agaibh?

Dhà, ceithir, a trì. Ceithir, neoni, neoni, a h-aon.

"What's your phone number?"
... Mr. MacLeod reads the new number from the phone
"243 4001."

Tioraidh!

Tapadh leibh.

As the policeman is saying goodbye, Tigger walks back in
"Goodbye!"
"Thank-you."

Dhà, trì, a ceithir. Naoi, naoi, naoi, a naoi.

While Mrs MacLeod is tidying up, she finds a leaflet for a temping agency, with phone number "234 9999", and decides to apply for a job

Màiri Anna... Mary Anne MacLeod.

Mrs MacLeod has gone for an interview and gives her name nervously in a mixture of English and Gaelic

Màiri Anna NicLeòid... Cò às a tha sibh?

A Leòdhas. Cò às a tha sibh fèin?

The receptionist speaks Gaelic and asks
"Where are you from?"
"From Lewis. Where do <u>you</u> come from?"

A Tiriodh!

"From Tiree!"

O! Tha Gàidhlig agaibh!

Mrs MacLeod? Feasgar math!

Mr Mackie arrives to interview Mrs MacLeod
"Mrs MacLeod? Good afternoon!"
"Oh! You speak Gaelic!"

Glè mhath!

Beagan. Tha mi ag ionnsachadh bhon telebhisean le 'Speaking Our Language.'

"A little. I'm learning from the television with Speaking Our Language."
"Very good!"

Ceart ma-tha.

"Right then."
He asks Mrs MacLeod to come through for an interview.

Tapadh leibh, Mrs MacLeod. Feasgar math.

The interview has not gone well. Mrs MacLeod is depressed
"Thank you Mrs MacLeod. Good afternoon."

Mrs MacLeod comes home, tired after the interview
"I want a cup of coffee!"

The children want something too!
"What do you want?"   "Chop Suey."

"Please!"

Eilidh repeats
"Please!"

Mr. MacLeod reluctantly agrees to go for the takeaway

However, he is side-tracked…

…and goes to the pub instead
The sign says: "Come in".

"Good evening, Iain. What do you want?"
"I would like a pint of lager, please."

Mr MacLeod arrives home at last with the takeaway
"Do you like Chop Suey?"

"Do you like coke?"

"Yes, I do!"

But next morning at breakfast, everyone is miserable
"I don't like waffles."   "I don't like tomato."

"I don't like cooking."

"I don't like Glasgow. I don't like Glasgow at all!"

But later Eilidh phones a friend
"… Fine! I like Glasgow …"

And that afternoon, friends call. Eilidh asks
"Do you like tenpin bowling?"   "We do."

"Hallò, a Ghranaidh."

"Hallò, Lesley. Ciamar a tha thu an diugh, a ghràidh?"

Mrs MacLeod is in a park, and watches a family meeting up
"Hello, Granny." "Hello, Lesley. How are you today, dear?"

"Tapadh leat, a ghràidh. Math, math!"

The child offers Granny a sweet
"Thank you dear. Yum, yum!"

C AT HOME AIG AN TAIGH

"Hallò. Feasgar math."

"Hallò. Tha i brèagha an-diugh."

Granny comes over to speak to Mrs MacLeod
"Hello. Good afternoon". "Hello. It's lovely today."

"Tha, tha clann agam. Mac agus nighean."

"A bheil clann agaibh?"

They watch the children and Granny asks
"Do you have children?" "Yes, I have children. A son and a daughter."

"A! – Dithis. Nighean agus balach?"

Mrs MacLeod takes out her childrens' photos and Granny puts on her glasses for a better look
"Ah – two. A girl and a boy?"

"Nighean agus balach. Eilidh agus Eòghann."

Mrs MacLeod takes the photos back to muse over
"A girl and a boy. Eilidh and Ewen."

"A Ghranaidh! Greasaibh oirbh."

The children have become impatient
"Granny! Hurry up."

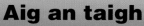

"Tìoraidh."

Granny says goodbye to Mrs MacLeod

Mrs MacLeod is at home in the kitchen studying her Highway Code

Eilidh comes in
" What's the time?" "It's nearly one o'clock."

"When's the film on? "
They take a look   "At two o'clock."

Mr MacLeod comes in
"What time is it?" "One o'clock."

Next, Ewen arrives
"When's the football on?"
"The football's on at two o'clock, son."

Ewen goes and settles himself in front of the TV to wait for the football. Eventually, he calls
"Daddy, hurry up. It's half past one."

His dad arrives, but falls asleep on the sofa and has to be wöken by Ewen
"Daddy! It's nearly two o'clock".

But Eilidh gets in first and changes channels for the film!

Dè an obair a th' agaibh, a Charol?

'S e clèireach a th' annam.

Mrs MacLeod is entertaining a new neighbour, whom she's met while gardening
"What do you do, Carol?" "I'm a secretary."

A! Clèireach. Càit a bheil sibh ag obair?

Tha mi ag obair ann an Comar nan Allt.

"Ah! A secretary. Where do you work?"
"I work in Cumbernauld".

Agus a bheil clann agaibh?

Chan eil fhathast.

"And do you have children?" (Carol is pregnant) "Not yet."

A Charol! Hallò. Feasgar math. Seo Iain.

A few days later, the MacLeods invite Carol and her husband for dinner   "Carol! Hello. Good evening. This is Iain."

Hai. Feasgar math. Is mise Carol, Iain. Agus seo Bill.

Carol introduces herself to Iain MacLeod
"Hi, good evening. I'm Carol, Iain. And this is Bill."

Dè an obair a th'agad, Bill?

Tha mi ag obair ann am banca. Dè an obair a th' agad fhèin, Iain?

Tha mi ag obair aig B.T.

At dinner the men chat about work in an informal way
"What do you do, Bill?"   "I work in a bank. What do you do yourself, Iain?"   " I work for B.T."

Agus Màiri Anna. Dè an obair a th' agad, a Mhàiri Anna?

The conversation moves to Mrs MacLeod
"And Mary Anne. What do you do?"

O! Tha mi gun obair an-dràsda.

"Oh! I'm unemployed just now."

GAELIC ORIGINS

Gaelic is a Celtic language whose earliest roots lie in central Europe. It was first brought to this country by settlers from the Antrim area of Ireland, known as *Gaidheil*.

The *Gaidheil* began arriving on the West coast of Scotland as early as the third century, when they established the kingdom of Dalriada in Argyll.

These early settlers were known to the Romans as 'Scotti' and it was one of the Scots' kings, Kenneth mac Alpin, who first united the Picts and the Scots in 843 AD. It was the Scots, too, who in the eleventh century established the kingdom now known as Scotland – and gave it its name.

As well as bringing Gaelic, the *Gaidheil* also brought Christianity to most of Scotland through the teachings of St. Columba and his followers, who made their base on the island of Iona.

As might be expected from its history, modern Scottish Gaelic is most closely related to Irish, but also has close links with Manx Gaelic. These three languages are also related, but less closely, to the other Celtic languages – Welsh, Cornish and Breton (the language of Brittany in France).

Although the number of people speaking Gaelic has declined, it remains the everyday language of many people throughout Scotland.

Sabhal Mòr Ostaig

The Gaelic college on Skye, *Sabhal Mòr Ostaig* (the Great Barn of Ostaig), was established to offer young Gaelic speakers access, in their own language, to the skills and training needed to allow them to take part in the economic development of the Highlands and Islands.

Built in 1820, the converted farm steading which now houses the college was first used for short courses in Gaelic, piping and clarsach. The provision of short courses has expanded, with students from as far away as the United States and Australia now attending a comprehensive range of courses.

The College opened its doors to full-time students for the first time in October 1983 when its Higher National Diploma (HND) in Business and *Gaidhealtachd* (Gaeldom) Studies was validated. Since then, the College has expanded its full time courses to include both Higher National Certificate (HNC) and HND courses in Business Studies with *Gaidhealtachd* Studies, Information Technology or Office Technology. The College also offers a Post-graduate Diploma in Gaelic Broadcasting.

Courses are taught in Gaelic and now *Sabhal Mòr Ostaig* plans to extend its existing accommodation to include further teaching rooms, a language laboratory, offices and facilities for television production courses. In addition there will be residential accommodation for up to 35 students.

Staff at *Sabhal Mòr* stress the importance of building pride and self-confidence in students so that they can make a better contribution to the development of their own communities.

Competence in Gaelic and an appreciation of Highland history and culture are regarded as essentials at the College, and help to ensure that students are well-equipped for careers in the *Gaidhealtachd*. Graduates of *Sabhal Mòr Ostaig* are now involved in business and professional life throughout the Highlands and Islands.

Some prospective students take a look round the idyllically situated College

PERSONAL NAMES

Gaelic has a rich variety of personal names. Some of these are of native Gaelic origin, while others tell us about the close contact Gaelic has had at different times with the Norse, Scots and English languages. Others have come from the Bible. Still others have arisen due to fashions of the time. The names in the following section derive from Gaelic unless otherwise stated. English equivalent names are given in brackets, although some of these, like Eachann and Hector, have no direct linguistic connection with each other.

MEN'S NAMES

Ailean – thought to mean noble one (Alan)

Alasdair – originally from Greek, but became popular after the three Scottish kings known as Alexander

Anndra – from Greek: the apostle was adopted as the patron saint of Scotland in the 13th century (Andrew)

Aonghas – unique choice (Angus)

Cailean – a form of Calum (Colin)

Calum – from Gille-Chaluim, Servant of Columba. Calum is a version of the Latin word "columba", a dove. St. Columba is Calum Cille (the dove of the church) in Gaelic (Malcolm, Calum)

Coinneach – fair one (Kenneth)

Dàibhidh – beloved, from Hebrew (David)

Dòmhnall – world ruler (Donald)

Donnchadh – brown warrior (Duncan)

Dùghlas – black stream, used as a personal name since the 16th century (Douglas)

Dùghall – dark foreigner, originally applied to a Norwegian Viking, as opposed to a Danish one, "fionn-ghall", a fair foreigner (Dugald, Dougal)

Eachann – horse lord (Hector)

Eàirdsidh – from Archie

Eòghann – well-born, connected with the Welsh name Owen (Ewan, sometimes Hugh)

Fearchar – very dear one (Farquhar)

Fionnlagh – fair hero (Finlay)

Gilleasbaig – servant of the bishop (Archibald, also found in the surname Gillespie)

Iain – originally from Hebrew, God is gracious (Ian, Iain, John)

Iomhar – from Norse (Ivor)

Murchadh – sea-battler (Murdoch)

Niall – champion (Neil)

Pàdraig – originally from Latin, nobleman (Patrick)

Raghnall – ruler of counsel, from Norse

Ruairidh – mighty ruler, literally red king (Roderick, Rory, Derick)

Seumas – originally from Hebrew (James, Hamish)

Torcall – cauldron of Thor, the Norse god of war (Torquil)

Tormod – wrath of Thor, the Norse god of war (Norman)

Uilleam – ultimately from Old English, helmet of determination, literally will-helmet (William)

Uisdean – from Norse (Hugh)

WOMEN'S NAMES

Anna – originally from Hebrew, grace (Ann, Anne, Anna)

Barabal – meaning uncertain (Barbara)

Beathag – life-giver (Rebecca, Beth)

Cairistìona – originally from Latin, follower of Christ (Christine, Christina)

Catrìona – originally from Greek, pure one (Catherine, Katherine)

Ceit – from English (Kate)

Ciorstaidh – the equivalent of Kirsty

Criosaidh – the equivalent of Chrissie

Doileag – the feminine form of Dòmhnall

Ealasaid – originally from Hebrew, oath of God (Elizabeth, Elspeth)

Eilidh – originally from Greek, bright (Helen, Ellen, Elaine)

Fionnghal – fair shoulder (Flora)

Iseabail – from French (Isobel)

Mairead – from Greek, pearl (Margaret)

Màiri – from the Hebrew name, Miriam (Mary)

Mòr – meaning uncertain (Marion, Sarah)

Mòrag – a form of Mòr (Morag, Marion, Sarah)

Oighrig – from Norse (Effie, Euphemia, Erica)

Peigi – from English (Peggy)

Raonaid – from Norse (Rachel)

Seonag – meaning uncertain (Joan, Joanne)

Seònaid – originally from Hebrew, God is gracious (Janet)

Sìleas – thought to be from a Norman name (Julia, Cecilia)

Sìne – connected with the name Seònaid (Jean, Jane, Sheena)

Una – meaning uncertain (Una, Oonagh, Agnes, Winifred)

CLI

Comann an Luchd-Ionnsachaidh (CLI), the Association of Gaelic Learners, exists to support and encourage Gaelic learners throughout Britain and beyond. Its membership has increased rapidly over the years, reflecting the growing interest in Gaelic from all over the world.

CLI also runs clubs for learners in various parts of Scotland, where people can get together to converse in Gaelic and help each other towards fluency in the language.

SURNAMES

Gaelic surnames usually contain the name of the family ancestor, but sometimes they derive from occupations or positions, or physical or personal characteristics, while others derive from names of places.

The word Mac *means son in Gaelic. If you are a woman and your surname begins in* Mac, *use* Nic, *daughter, instead of* Mac *in the Gaelic version of your name – for example,* Alasdair MacLeòid *but* Màiri NicLeòid. *Surnames beginning in* Mac/Nic *are the most common type in Gaelic.*

Mac a' Ghobhainn – of the smith (Smith)

Mac a' Phearsain – of the parson (Macpherson)

MacAmhlaigh – of Amhlaigh, a Norse name (MacAulay)

Mac an Aba – of the abbot (MacNab)

Mac an t-Saoir – of the carpenter (Macintyre)

Mac an Tòisich – of the chief (Mackintosh)

MacAoidh – of Aodh, an old Gaelic name meaning fire (Mackay)

MacAonghais – of Aonghas (MacInnes)

MacArtair – of Artair (MacArthur)

MacAsgaill – of Asgaill, a Norse name (MacAskill)

MacCoinnich – of Coinneach (Mackenzie)

MacDhòmhnaill – of Dòmhnall (MacDonald)

MacDhonnchaidh – of Donnchadh (Robertson)

MacFhearghais – of Fearghas (Fergus), a Gaelic name meaning supreme choice (Ferguson)

MacGriogair – of Griogair (Gregor). Several saints bore the Latin form of this name, Gregorius (MacGregor)

MacIomhair – of Iomhar (Ivor) (MacIver)

MacLeòid – of Leòd (MacLeod)

MacMhathain – of the bear (Matheson)

MacNeacail – of Neacal (Nicol). The name Neacal, originally from Greek, became popular owing to the fame of St. Nicholas (Nicolson, MacNicol)

MacNèill – of Niall (MacNeill, MacNeil)

MacPhàil – of Pòl (Paul), from the name of the apostle (MacPhail)

MacRath – of grace (MacRae)

MacSuain – of Suain, a Norse name (MacSween)

MacThòmais – of Tòmas (Thomas), from the apostle's name, meaning twin (Thomson, Thompson)

A number of names contain the word "gille". It is often followed by the name of a saint , a Biblical figure or a church dignitary, and here meant "a follower or disciple". The letter g of gille is sometimes dropped in names of this type.

Gilleasbaig – of the bishop (Gillespie)

MacGilleBhrìghde – of St. Bridget (Gilbride)

MacGilleChrìosda – of Christ (Gilchrist)

MacGillEathain or **MacGill-Eain** – of Seathan (a form of John) (MacLean)

MacGilliosa – of Jesus (Gillies)

MacGilleMhìcheil - of the Archangel Michael (Carmichael)

MacGilleMhoire – of Mary (Gilmour)

Only a small proportion of names do not begin in Mac, Nic or Gille. Here is a short selection of those that don't:

Caimbeul – crooked mouth (Campbell)

Camshron – crooked nose (Cameron)

Friseal – a Norman name (Fraser)

Moireach – derived from the place name, Moray (Murray)

Stiùbhart – derived from King Robert II's position as High Steward of Scotland (Stewart, Stuart)

Urchardan – derived from the name of the place on Loch Ness-side (Urqhuart)

Sorley MacLean

Sorley MacLean – **Somhairle MacGill-Eain** in Gaelic – is the most famous Gaelic poet of the twentieth century and is recognised as one of the greatest Gaelic poets of all time.

Bàrdachd (poetry) has a particularly important part in Gaelic tradition and there have been many notable poets over the years. One of Sorley MacLean's greatest achievements has been to develop twentieth century themes in Gaelic poetry. He has written about the Spanish Civil War and poverty in the cities as well as on traditional themes like love, the landscape and the history and culture of the Highlands. His work has been translated into many languages and he has received recognition in many countries.

Many of Sorley MacLean's poems are now published with parallel English translations, making it possible for non-Gaelic speakers to gain an appreciation of his work.

AN ROGHAINN	THE CHOICE
Choisich mi cuide ri mo thuigse a-muigh ri taobh a' chuain; bha sinn còmhla ach bha ise a' fuireach tiotan bhuam.	I walked with my reason out beside the sea. We were together but it was keeping a little distance from me.

The beginning of this poem is reprinted by kind permission of the author.

Play Gaelic!

The Cròileagan (Gaelic playgroup) movement is one of the most exciting developments in Gaelic education today.

More than 1700 pre-school children now attend Gaelic playgroups and nurseries in most parts of Scotland. There are over 100 of these groups and new ones are being established every year.

The first cròileagan was set up in 1981 by Gaelic speaking parents who wanted their children to begin their education in a Gaelic

environment. The idea quickly became popular and many of the children who now attend a cròileagan come from non-Gaelic speaking families who appreciate the opportunity for children to become fluent in another language.

Comhairle nan Sgoiltean Araich (The Gaelic Pre-School Council) is the association that co-ordinates the setting up of new groups and provides support to the cròileagan movement. It runs toy libraries, resource centres, training courses for volunteers, parent and child groups and classes for non-Gaelic speaking parents who want to keep up with their children.

Gaelic playgroups and nursery schools are important in encouraging children to speak Gaelic and by educating the very young they are ensuring the future of the language.

The Spell of Words!

In recent years, there have been changes in the spelling of some Gaelic words to bring them into line with spelling conventions.

These conventions, (which can be obtained from the Scottish Examination Board, Ironmills Road, Dalkeith), aim to standardise Gaelic spelling. Most modern publications use the revised spellings.

One of the most obvious examples of the revised spelling is 'taigh', the word for house, although it can still be seen spelled

as 'tigh' all over the Highlands and Islands. According to the revised standards, the letter t followed by the vowels a, o or u is pronounced like the t in *tapadh leibh*. However, t followed by an i or e is pronounced like the t in *Tìoraidh*.

Examples of signs

Place names

Place names can tell us a great deal about the history of an area, town or village and the people who once lived there. A little research can be well worthwhile.

Many Scottish place names are Gaelic in origin, showing that Gaelic was once the language of the majority of people in most parts of Scotland, including places like Galloway and Ayrshire where virtually no Gaelic remains today.

The Gaelic words 'baile' (village or town), 'achadh' (field), 'cill' or 'cille' (church or religious settlement), 'dùn' (fort) and 'creag' (rock), frequently appear in Scottish place names, often slightly disguised or anglicised. Here are some examples:

‹ Creag an Iubhair

Baile – Ballachullish (town of the straits), Balallan (Ailean's town);

Achadh – Achmore (big field), Achnamara (field of the sea), Achnaba (field of the cow);

Dùn Breatainn

Cill – Kilmarnock (St. Marnock's church),Kilbride (St. Bridget's church), Kilbowie (yellow church);

Dùn – Dumbarton (fort of the Britons),Dunkeld (fort of the Caledonians), Dunbeg (small fort);

Creag – Craigentinny (rock of the fox), Craignure (yew rock), Craigmillar (rock of the millar).

Geographical features like lochs, mountains and rocks often have descriptive Gaelic names, for example *Creag na h-Iolaire*, 'eagle's rock'. Others may tell a story as in *Beinn na Caillich* (on Skye), 'old woman's mountain',

Baile a' Chaolais ›

supposedly named after a princess buried at the summit, or *Loch nan Dàl* (again, on Skye), 'loch of waiting', where ships used to shelter during stormy weather.

Of course, not all Scottish names derive from Gaelic and even in the Highlands there are many names of other origins. Perhaps the most common of these are Norse names, brought to Scotland by the Vikings when they colonised much of North and West Scotland. Norse names are particularly numerous in Shetland, Orkney and Caithness but are also found extensively in Skye and the Western Isles.

Cille Bhrìghde an Ear

Examples are words ending in 'aig' or 'wick' – bay, such as Mallaig and Wick, or 'bost',– farm (N. bolstadr) such as Shawbost.

Runrig

One of the most familiar and popular images of modern Scottish Gaeldom is the musical group Runrig. The group, who include in their repertoire many Gaelic songs (both traditional and of their own composition), were formed by musicians from Skye and North Uist in 1973. Their subsequent development has coincided with a general resurgence of interest throughout Scotland (and beyond) in the Gaelic language and culture. In many instances, that interest can be attributed to Runrig's music and public performances, as many young people have been introduced to the Gaelic language through their recordings.

Their first album 'Play Gaelic' was released in 1978 and 1991 saw their seventh album release 'The Big Wheel' – *An Cuibhle Mòr*. The single from that album, 'Hearthammer', entered the UK singles chart in September 1991, when they were reviewed by the Sunday Times newspaper as 'The world's foremost Gaelic rock band'.

The group's name denotes a system of joint tenancy in agriculture, and combines the Gaelic word *roinn* (division) and the Scots word *rig* (strip of ploughed land).

PATRONYMICS – Family Ties!

We've already had a look at Gaelic surnames, but in Gaelic communities people are sometimes known rather differently. The man known as John MacDonald to his city workmates could also be known as Iain mac Alasdair mhic Sheumais – *Iain son of Alasdair son of James,–* or Iain Alasdair Sheumais *for short.* You may have heard something like this in the Runrig song Sìol Ghoraidh.

Patronymics are a useful way of identifying people in areas where many people have the same names, but they also highlight the importance that most Gaels place on family ties. Some people can name their ancestors a long way back using the skill of sloinneadh. *(The word* sloinneadh *is also used to mean surname in some areas.)*

Nick–names are also popular in Gaelic communities and are often incorporated in patronymics. Sometimes these describe a personal characteristic, e.g. Anna Bhàn, *fair-haired Anna, or* Màiri Mhòr, *big Mary. On other occasions they refer to an occupation, e.g.* Seumas Nèill a' chìobair, *James son of Neil the shepherd, or to a person's origins, e.g.* Iain Hearach, *literally John, the Harrisman.*

Comunn na Gàidhlig

Comunn na Gàidhlig (CNAG) was established in 1984 as a coordinating development agency for Gaelic.

It is mainly funded through the Scottish Education Department in recognition of the importance of education to the Gaelic language and culture.

When it was first set up, CNAG concentrated its activity on education, the arts and the media. These initiatives have produced many excellent results, such as the growth of schools offering education through the medium of Gaelic.

While continuing to operate in these areas, CNAG has now undertaken additional commitments. These include extending the role of Gaelic in social and economic development and encouraging companies and organisations to adopt a bilingual approach to their business activities.

Shinty

The game of shinty (known in Gaelic as *camanachd,* or *iomain*) is very popular in many of the Highland and Gaelic-speaking areas of Scotland. Fast-moving and definitely only for the fit, it is quite similar to the Irish game of hurling and is said to have been used as an exercise for battle by the Celtic warriors of old!

In spite of its warlike ancestry, shinty today is an amateur sport famous for its friendly spirit and the community support which its main teams enjoy. It is played with 12 men on each side, in a season that lasts from August/September to June/July. The most important match of the season is the Camanachd Cup whose winners are regarded as the Scottish champions.

THE NEVIS RANGE

Scotland's newest ski resort is also home to the country's only cable-car system on *Aonach Mòr* near Fort William.

The Nevis Range at the 4,006 foot *Aonach Mòr* (Gaelic meaning – the large mountain top) offers 19 different ski-runs ranging from easy to difficult, while the new sport of snowboarding – surfing on snow on a single extra-wide ski – has become popular with many skiers visiting the area.

The cable-car system at *Aonach Mòr* has 80 gondolas which run for 45 weeks of the year. In the summer, climbers and walkers replace the skiers, taking well marked footpaths to the viewpoints of *Meall Beag* and *Sgurr Finnisgaig* where they can enjoy views over the Western Highlands from Loch Linnhe to Loch Lochy.

Aonach Mòr is more than just a sports playground, however. It is also of considerable environmental importance and planners have recognised the necessity of maintaining the mountain's wildlife and vegetation as well as developing its leisure facilities.

The Snowgoose Bowl on the upper part of the mountain provides a breeding ground for dotterel and is therefore protected as a Site of Special Scientific Interest. Buzzards and eagles can also be seen there. Although conditions in this area are harsh, slow-growing plants can survive and so the vegetation includes many attractive mosses and liverworts.

The developers aim to make the mountain accessible to all, without destroying its unique environment.

Listen to your radio...

A wide variety of Gaelic radio progammes can be heard all over Scotland and many learners have found them a useful way of becoming more familiar with the language and increasing their vocabulary.

The most popular Scotland-wide programmes are Na Naidheachdan, *(the News)*, Aithris an Fheasgair, *(Evening Report)* and Na Dùrachdan, *(music requests programme).*

There are also conversation pieces, programmes on music and the arts and a weekly church service, Dèanamaid Adhradh, *(Let us Worship).*

Listeners to Radio nan Gaidheal *(Radio Highland).* and Radio nan Eilean *(the Western Isles radio service)* have an even wider choice, with programmes ranging from morning news reports to pop shows.

VIKING MICE

Researchers studying the evidence of Viking settlement on Hiort (St. Kilda) have found an unlikely ally in the island's humble field-mouse.

Genetic studies have shown that the long-tailed St. Kildan mouse (apodemus sylvaticus hirtensis) is more closely related to Norwegian mice than to its cousins on the British mainland.

This may mean that these mice arrived in Viking longships.

A GOOD READ

The Gaelic Books Council was set up in 1968, with the aid of a Scottish Education Department grant, in order to support and stimulate Gaelic publishing. It has done this by grant-assisting individual Gaelic books, commissioning authors and holding literary competitions.

The Council also publicises and catalogues all Gaelic and Gaelic-related books, while at the same time providing general literary advice and an editorial service, as well as selling books both by post and direct to the public through a wide variety of venues and events.

The Gaelic Books Council is now funded by the Scottish Arts Council. More details of its work may be found in the Gaelic Books Council's Annual Report, available free from its office at: The Department of Celtic, University of Glasgow, Glasgow G12 8Q9

A selection of publications with Gaelic text

The Other Gaidhealtachd?

Cape Breton Island, part of the Canadian province of Nova Scotia, has on occasion been referred to as 'the other Gaidhealtachd'. The East coast of the North American continent might seem an unlikely place for such a community - how did Cape Breton earn this description?

Cape Breton's *Gàidhealtachd* (Gaeldom) was first created in the eighteenth and nineteenth centuries by Scottish emigrants who established Gaelic-speaking communities in their new country. Five or six generations later, you can still meet Cape Bretoners like Calum Smith who lives in Sydney, Cape Breton's major city, whose Gaelic is still just as fluent as was his Lewis ancestors'!

Cape Breton's charm attracts many visitors every year

Perhaps the most interesting thing about Cape Breton is the way its Gaelic culture has developed independently over the last two hundred years, even although the number of Gaelic speakers has declined since the first emigrants settled there. Cape Breton's distinctive music and literature draw on Cape Bretoners' own experiences, with little reference to the Scottish Highlands, even though both share the same Gaelic roots and language.

There are still similarities, however. Like Scotland, Cape Breton Island is a strikingly beautiful place with magnificent scenery. Like Scotland too, its young people are developing an awareness of their own heritage and a renewed interest in the Gaelic language. It is now confidently predicted that there will be more people speaking Gaelic in Cape Breton in thirty years' time than there are today. The dynamic young Rankin Family, whose Cape Breton style of Gaelic music is becoming increasingly popular in Scotland as well as in Canada, is a good example of this new trend.

It is not surprising then that many people in Scotland's *Gaidhealtachd* are looking with interest at these lively developments in Cape Breton.

THE BRAHAN SEER

Gaelic tradition is rich in stories and legends , many of them handed down by word of mouth through the generations, and many concerning the gift of second sight. Some of the most famous of these stories centre on a shadowy figure, called the Brahan Seer, known in Gaelic as *Coinneach Odhar* (Sallow Kenneth).

Tradition tells us that *Coinneach Odhar* lived in the seventeenth century (though some sources place him earlier). He travelled throughout the Highlands and made a large number of prophecies, many of which have been fulfilled – for example the Highland Clearances and the emigrations which resulted. The building of the Caledonian Canal was another prophecy that came true.

Coinneach Odhar's prophecies are still remembered and talked about in the Highlands today. A significant event, such as an accident or the washing away of a bridge, can revive memories of *Coinneach*'s prophecies– although as with all prophets there is sometimes doubt as to whether or not his prophecies have been fulfilled. It all depends on the interpretation.

One of *Coinneach*'s most famous prophecies - the eventual downfall of the Seaforth MacKenzies - proved to be fatal for himself. Tradition tells us that he met his death when the offended Lady Seaforth had him thrown into a barrel of burning tar studded with spikes.

The Caledonian Canal prophecy

"Thig an latha sam faicear làraichean Sasannach air an tarraing le srianan corcaich seachad air cùl Tom na h-Iùbhraich"

Profile of a Gaelic Learner

Alasdair Màrtainn (Martin) is a fluent Gaelic speaker who lives in Breakish on the Isle of Skye. Unlike many fluent speakers, however, he is an adult learner of Gaelic. How did he achieve fluency?

Alasdair grew up on Lochness-side where Gaelic was spoken only by a few elderly people. Although he remembers having Gaelic-speaking uncles, he had no Gaelic as a child and there was none in his home. It was not until many years later that Alasdair became interested in learning Gaelic, whilst living in Easter Ross.

Like many other successful adult learners, Alasdair used a variety of methods, seizing every opportunity to develop his language skills. He attended night classes to acquire the basics, then joined a group of learners in a conversation class led by fluent native speakers. Alasdair reinforced his progress at residential Gaelic courses and quickly reached Higher grade standard with proficiency.

Alasdair's growing interest in Gaelic eventually led to a career change, when he secured a scholarship at Sabhal Mòr Ostaig for a two year business studies course. He moved to Skye with his family, and now along with his wife, Christine, runs a successful business from home, publishing and marketing books and tapes of traditional music.

Alasdair's family are now learning Gaelic too! He has four children and the two youngest will complete their primary schooling through the medium of Gaelic at Broadford Primary School.

Alasdair and Christine with two of their children

 # The Mòd

The annual National *Mòd*, which in 1992 received the accolade of Royal status *(Am Mòd Naiseanta Rìoghail)*, is Scotland's major festival of the Gaelic arts , where hundreds of competitors try themselves out in over 130 competitions. The musical competitions range from solo voice, part-singing and choral music, to instrumental music on pipe, fiddle, clarsach, piano or accordion. There are also competitions for folk groups. Gaelic Literary competitions include recitation, drama and composition of prose and poetry.

The *Mòd* was conceived just over one hundred years ago by *An Comunn Gàidhealach*, – The Highland Association. *An Comunn* was founded in 1891 by a small core of Gaelic devotees who were deeply concerned for the future of the language and realised the need for a formal body to restore some of the confidence eroded by centuries of hardship and oppression. *An Comunn*'s early aim was to promote and preserve Gaelic in the arts, in local industry and especially in education and it adopted as its motto: *Ar Cànain 's Ar Ceòl* - Our Language and Our Music.

An Comunn's first project was to launch a national festival modelled on the thriving Welsh 'Eisteddfod'. The first *Mòd* offered 10 competitions and lasted only one day, but this has grown over a century into the major national event that we know today, complete with an extensive fringe of ceilidhs and concerts by Gaelic personalities and musicians as well as a network of smaller 'local' mòds throughout the country.

Young people are an important part of the Mòd's activities

The *Mòd* takes place at a different venue each year. Oban, which hosted the very first *Mòd*, has been the most popular rendezvous, closely followed by Glasgow. All of Scotland's major towns have played host at some time, including Edinburgh, Aberdeen, Dundee and Inverness in the East, and Stornoway and Dunoon in the West.

A young piper is put through his paces.

Gaelic speakers and learners now have a greater choice of television viewing than ever before. Highlights of the programmes funded by *Comataidh Telebhisein Gàidhlig* include the Gaelic 'soap' *Machair*, news bulletins and documentaries whose subjects range from Scottish history to life in our cities today.

The new Gaelic programmes aren't just confined to Scottish topics however. There's also a series about music from all over the world, presented in Gaelic, and a series on European issues affecting Scotland.

Look out for these and other programmes. Many of them carry subtitles, so even if you haven't advanced too far with your Gaelic you should still be able to enjoy them!

TURSACHAN CHALANAIS
THE STONES OF CALLANISH

On a ridge overlooking Loch Roag in Lewis, not far from the village of Callanish, stands one of the greatest prehistoric monuments in Europe, the Stones of Callanish. These impressive 'megaliths', rivals to Stonehenge, are believed to date from three or four thousand years ago when they were built by the pre-Celtic, Neolithic (New Stone Age) inhabitants of the island.

The Stones, often known as *Na Fir Bhrèige* – The False Men – number more than fifty and form a cross shape from North to South, 400 feet long by 150 feet wide. Several other circles exist within three miles of Callanish.The stones vary in height from 3.5 to 15.5 feet and are arranged in a central circle with five lines of stones radiating outwards, two of which form an avenue to the central circle. Inside the circle is a tall central pillar which is believed by some to have been used in human sacrifice during ancient religious ceremonies. Others assert that the site was a burial ground, and archaeologists have discovered the remains of a burial chamber within the circle, containing evidence of cremation.

Extensive research has been carried out to explore the theory that the monument's original function was as an astronomical observatory to allow the movement of sun, moon and stars to be studied. Evidence for this has been found in the Stones' remarkably accurate alignment. The real purpose of the Stones, however, is still the subject of controversy after more than a century of research.

The enigma of *Tursachan Chalanais* continues to perplex and fascinate scholars, and their mystic beauty attracts large numbers of sightseers every year. Now visitors can even enjoy a cup of tea in the nearby restored black-house while they shelter a while from the chilling Lewis wind!

FLORA MACDONALD

A heroine of Scottish history, Flora MacDonald owes her fame to the help she gave Charles Edward Stewart in his escape to France after the defeat of the Jacobites at Culloden in 1746.

The Prince had managed to escape to the Western Isles after the battle, but because of the danger and failure to secure a sea passage to France, Flora MacDonald took the Prince, disguised as her maid, from Uist to Skye and then to Raasay, from whence the Prince finally made his escape to France.

Flora MacDonald was born in Milton in South Uist, while her husband came from Kingsburgh in Skye. The couple emigrated to North Carolina in 1774, only to face tragedy when her family supported the losing side in the American War of Independence.

She later returned to Skye to die, and is buried at Kilmuir.

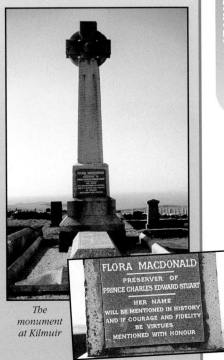

The monument at Kilmuir

FLORA MACDONALD
PRESERVER OF
PRINCE CHARLES EDWARD STUART
HER NAME
WILL BE MENTIONED IN HISTORY
AND IF COURAGE AND FIDELITY
BE VIRTUES
MENTIONED WITH HONOUR

à-à-à accents

Gaelic uses a mark called a grave accent over vowels in some words to show that they should be lengthened in sound.

Gaelic is similar to many other languages in using extra symbols. It is worth noting that the *grave* accent in Gaelic (which slopes down towards the end of a word, for example *càr*) is not shown on capital letters. This can be confusing when pronouncing proper names. For example, Islay is just spelt *Ile*, but the i is lengthened (ee-luh) even though the accent is not shown.

Until recently, two accents were used in Gaelic. The acute accent (which sloped the other way) has been discarded and only the grave accent is now used. Many books and dictionaries still in print, however, show both accents.

Children's ditties
Rannan beaga chloinne

Although these rhymes are meant for children, they are excellent for Gaelic learners of all ages!
A rough translation is provided for each one.

Mo, Mo, Mo, Chunnaic Mise Bò!

Mo, mo, mo, chunnaic mise bò
Shìos air cùl a' ghàrraidh, mo, mo, mo.

Woo, woo, woo, chuala mise cù
Bha e 'g ithe cnàmhan, woo, woo, woo.

Miau, miau, miau, ars an cat 's e 'g iarraidh
Iasg airson a dhiathad, miau, miau, miau.

Thuirt an coileach gog 'nuair a fhuair e sgleog
'S bha a' chearc a' gàgail, gog, gog-gog, gog-gog.

Mea, mea, mea, ars an t-uan an-dè
'S e air call a mhàthair, mea, mea, mea.

Iho, ars an t-each, 's ruith Iain beag a-steach
'G èigheachd mòr ri mhàthair, O, mo chreach, mo chreach.

Moo, Moo, Moo, I Saw a Cow!

Moo, moo, moo, I saw a cow
Down beyond the garden, moo, moo, moo.

Woo, woo, woo, I heard a dog
He was eating bones, woo, woo, woo.

Mew, mew, mew, said the cat demanding
Fish for his dinner, mew, mew, mew.

The cock said gog, when he got a shock
And the hen was clucking, gog, gog-gog, gog-gog.

Maa, maa, maa, the lamb said yesterday
When he lost his mother, maa, maa, maa.

Neigh, went the horse, Iain ran into the house
Shouting to his mother, Oh dear, Oh dear, Oh dear.

Aon, Dhà, Trì

Aon, dhà, trì,
An cat, an cù 's mi fhìn;
Ruith 's a' leum air feadh a ghàrraidh
Gus a fàs sinn sgìth.

Ceithir, còig, sia,
Uisg neo gaoth neo fèath.
Togaidh sinne bothan beag
Le clachan agus criadh.

Seachd, ochd, naoi,
Gheibh mi slat is sreang
'S thèid mi dh' iasgach anns an abhainn
Gus an tig an oidhch'.

Deich 's a h-aon deug,
Chan e facal brèig
Gun do chunnt mi fichead starrag
'S iad 'na suidh' air geug.

Source: Màiri Tàilleir, Rannan Eibhinn Cloinne,
Gairm: Leabhar 16, Glasgow (1969).

One, Two, Three

One, two, three,
The dog, the cat and me;
Running, leaping round the garden
Until we grow tired.

Four, five, six,
Rain or wind or calm.
We will build a little hut
With pebbles and with clay.

Seven, eight, nine,
I'll take a rod and string
And I'll go fishing in the river
Until night comes.

Ten and eleven,
It wouldn't be a lie
If I said I counted twenty crows
Sitting on a branch.

Na Corragan

An òrdag, an sgealbag,
An gunna fada, Mac an Aba,
Agus lùdag bheag an airgid.

The Fingers

Thumb, index finger,
The long gun (middle finger), the abbot's son (ring finger),
And the little money finger ('pinkie').

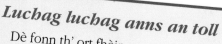

Luchag luchag anns an toll

Dè fonn th' ort fhèin
A chait chaoil ghlais
Mharbh thu mo mhàthair an-dè
Is thàr mi fhèin air èiginn às

Little mouse, little mouse in the hole

What's your own tune
Thin grey cat?
You murdered my mother yesterday
And I only just escaped myself.

Here are the words of some popular Gaelic songs – why not listen out for them on the radio?
An English version is provided for each song, although most people agree that the Gaelic versions sound much better!

'S ann an Ile

Seist

'S ann an Ile, 'n Ile, 'n Ile,
'S ann an Ile rugadh mi.
'S ann an Ile, 'n Ile, 'n Ile,
'S ann an Ile bhòidheach.

Rannan

'S ann an Ile ghorm an fheòir
A rugadh mi 's a thogadh mi,
'S ann an Ile ghorm an fheòir
A rugadh mi 's a bha mi.

'S ann an Ile bhòidheach
A rugadh mi 's a thogadh mi,
'S ann an Ile bhòidheach
A rugadh mi 's a bha mi.

Nuair a bha mi ann an Ile
Bha Catrìona cuide rium,
Nuair a bha mi ann an Ile
Bha Catrìona comh' rium.

Am measg nam bruachan
        bòidheach, buidhe,
Bha Catrìona cuide rium,
Am measg nam bruachan
        bòidheach, buidhe,
Bha Catrìona comh' rium.

A traditional 'Port a Beul', mouth-music. This type of song was made by fitting light-hearted, often nonsensical, words to traditional pipe and fiddle tunes. It is thought that this came about as a result of legislation passed in 1746 proscribing the use of bagpipes – so people danced to the songs instead of to music.

It Was in Islay

Chorus:
It was in Islay, Islay, Islay
It was in Islay I was born
It was in Islay, Islay, Islay
It was in beautiful Islay.

Verses:
It was in Islay, green of grass
That I was born and raised
It was in Islay, green of grass
That I was born and lived.

It was in beautiful Islay
That I was born and raised
It was in beautiful Islay
That I was born and lived.

When I was in Islay
Catrìona was along with me
When I lived in Islay
Catrìona was with me.

Among the bonny, yellow hills
Catrìona was along with me
Among the bonny, yellow hills
Catrìona was with me.

Dòmhnall Beag an t-Siùcair

Seist

Dòmhnall beag an t-siùcair
an t-siùcair, an t-siùcair
Dòmhnall beag an t-siùcair
Is dùil aige pòsadh.

Rannan

Cha ghabh a' chlann nighean e
Chlann nighean e, chlann nighean e
Cha ghabh a' chlann nighean e
Bho'n nach eil e bòidheach.

Ged a bhiodh na ginidhean
Na ginidhean, na ginidhean
Ged a bhiodh na ginidhean
A' gliogadaich na phòcaid.

Another popular 'Port a Beul' with amusing lyrics and a catchy tune, known to musicians as 'The High Road to Linton'.

Wee Donald of the Sugar

Chorus:
Wee Donald of the sugar
The sugar, the sugar
Wee Donald of the sugar
He's looking for a bride

Verses:
The young girls won't have him
won't have him, won't have him
The young girls won't have him
Because he isn't handsome.

Although he would have guineas
Have guineas, have guineas
Although he would have guineas
Jingling in his pockets

Fear a' Bhàta

Seist

Fhir a' bhàta, 's na ho ro eile,
Fhir a' bhàta, 's na ho ro eile,
Fhir a' bhàta, 's na ho ro eile,
Mo shoraidh slàn leat, gach àit' an tèid thu.

Rannan

'S tric mi sealltainn o'n chnoc a's àirde,
Feuch am faic mi fear a' bhàta,
An tig thu an-diugh, no'n tig thu a-màireach?
'S mur tig thu idir gur truagh a tà mi.

Tha mo chridhe-sa briste, brùite
'S tric na deòir a' ruith o'm shùilean.
An tig thu a-nochd, no am bidh mo dhùil riut,
No'n dùin mi'n dorus le osna thùrsaich?

'S tric mi foighneachd de luchd nam bàta
Am fac iad thu, no am bheil thu sàbhailt'?
Ach 's ann a tha gach aon dhiubh 'g ràitinn
Gur gòrach mise, ma thug mi gràdh dhuit.

A lament for a lost lover, author unknown.

NOTE:'Na ho ro eile' is made of meaningless vocables, like 'fa la la' etc. in English

Oh Boat Man

Chorus:
Oh boat man, na ho ro eile, (3 times)
My blessing with you where e're you go.

Verses:
Often I search from the highest hill,
To try if I can see the boat man.
Will you come today, or come tomorrow?
If you don't come, wretched am I.

O my heart is bruised and broken
And oft' the tears run from my eyes.
Will you come tonight, can I expect you,
Or close the door with a sorrowful sigh?

Often I ask of the boat crews
If they have seen you, or are you safe?
But each one of them says
That I was foolish to love you.

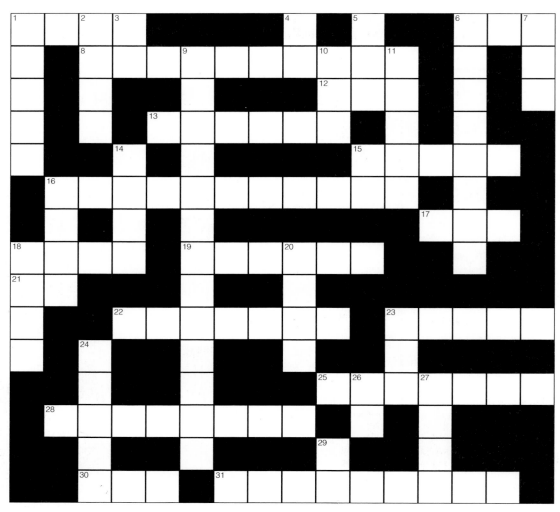

All the answers to this puzzle are in Gaelic. You may not have come across *all* the vocabulary yet, but with a bit of thought and perhaps some help from a friend, you should be able to complete it! The answers are at the bottom of the page if you get *really* stuck.

Tarsainn

1. The opposite of hot (4)
6 … *an taigh*. At home (3)
8. Germany. *a'*......... (10)
12. Not what you breathe <u>on</u> (3)
13. How? (6)
15. Where? (5)
16. Often accompanies a meal (7, 4)
17. See *20 sìos*
18. ...... *mo leisgeul!* (4)
19. Makes things sweeter (6)
21. Drink! (2)
22. *Seachd deug + trì* (7)
23. See *25 tarsainn*
25. & 23. Good morning (7, 5)
28. *Ochd + naoi + dhà* (4, 4)
30. Without (3)
31. *An* .... *Addams.* A TV creepy bunch! (9)

Sìos

1. Vegetarians don't eat this. (5)
2. And. (4)
3. The Queen's lost two letters (*a' bhàn_ig_*). (2)
4. Midday. ...... *uair dheug.* (2)
5. A Gaelic learners' group that's left.(3)
6. In the casebook, Finlay was this. (2,6)
7. & 23. T Is this whisky very good? (3,5)
9. You are learning Gaelic. *Tha mi … ......*(2,11)
10. West. (3)
11. Terminates at Queen Street. (5)
14. The opposite of *dona*. (4)
15. Who? (2)
16. The colour of bog cotton. (4)
18. Elvis's suede shoes were this. (4)
20. & 17. T The negative response to *A bheil?* (4, 3)
23. Was Royal in 1992 for the first time. (3)
24. The colour of Burns's love. (5)
26. *Dè … uair a tha e ?* (2)
27. Girl's name. (4)
29. … *òl.* Drinking.(2)

Scotland
Alba

The Speaking Our Language TV programmes were filmed at different locations which you can see pictured here. You'll also notice from our map that many Scottish place names are Gaelic in origin, while others often have a Gaelic version.

Na Hearadh

Leòdhas

Arcaibh

Uibhist a Tuath

Port Rìgh

• Tunga

Inbhir Uige •

Leòdhas   Steòrnabhagh •   • Loch an Inbhir

Na Hearadh   Goillspidh •

Uibhist a Tuath

Port Rìgh •

Uibhist a Deas   **An t-Eilean Sgitheanach**   • An Caol   **Inbhir Nis** •

An Caol

Barraigh •   Rùm •

ALBA

Obar Dheathain •

Èige •

Eilean nam Muc

Colla •   • An Gearasdan

Tiriodh •

Muile   **Dùn Dèagh** •

• An t-Oban   Peairt •

Dùn Eideann

Uibhist a Deas

Colbhasa •   • Sruighlea

Diùra •   **Dùn Eideann** •

Ile   **Glaschu**

Arainn

Sruighlea

Glaschu

Do you understand?
A bheil thu a' tuigsinn?

TIME TO TRANSLATE

All the phrases below have appeared somewhere in the study pack. See how many you can understand – **without** looking them up!

Dè an uair a tha e?

....

Tha i brèagha!

....

Tha mi ag iarraidh cupa tì.

....

Càit a bheil sibh a' fuireach?

....

Is toigh leam snàmh.

....

'S e saor a th' annam.

....

A bheil clann agaibh?

....

Cuin a tha a' bhùth a' fosgladh?

....

Tha e dà uair.

....

Tha an dìnnear deiseil.

....

Càit a bheil do chòta, a ghràidh?

....

Dè an t-ainm a th' oirbh?

....

Gabh mo leisgeul!

....

Cupa cofaidh le bainne, mas e ur toil e.

....

Dè an seòladh a th' agaibh?

....

Seo an nighean agam.

....

TURN THE TABLES

Now translate the following English phrases into Gaelic. When asking a question, assume that you are talking to another adult, unless otherwise specified.

How are you today?

....

I don't like coffee.

....

This is my husband.

....

Where do you work just now?

....

I live in Glasgow.

....

One o'clock.

....

I have two sons and a daughter.

....

Good morning!

....

What's your phone number?

....

335 7012.

....

Where's your jumper, dear? (To a child)

....

I am unemployed.

....

Let's go!

....

When does the bus leave?

....

I work in a bank.

....

Good night!

....

Did you enjoy the soup?

....

It's a pleasure.

....

On these pages we've included notes on some of the main points that puzzle learners. You may have met some of them already in 'Ceum air Cheum' or 'Oisean an Teaghlaich' – but a fuller explanation is provided here.

AN AIBIDIL – THE ALPHABET

An important thing to remember about Gaelic is that it has a different alphabet. Instead of having 26 letters as in English, there are only 18. But what Gaelic lacks in letters, it makes up for in sounds – as you've no doubt realised!

The letters of the Gaelic alphabet are:

A B C D E F G H I L
M N O P R S T U

Although the letters themselves are not used, you often hear sounds like J, K, V and Y in Gaelic words.

So, where do they come from? Generally, they are produced by the letters or combinations of letters shown below.

J   **d** followed by **i** or **e**:
dè? – what?

Dè?

K   **c** followed by **i** or **e**:
ciamar? – how?

V   **bh** or **mh**.
glè mhath – very good

But be on your guard when these letters appear in the middle of a word. They may sound more like a **w** or they may not be sounded at all

MacAmhlaigh – MacAulay (w sound)
Inbhir Nis – Inverness (bh not sounded)

Tha Caisteal Inbhir Nis glè mhath!

Y   **dh** followed by **i** or **e** :
dh'ith – ate

Note that the Q, X and Z sounds are rare in Gaelic, as is a W sound at the beginning of a word. All of these normally occur only in borrowed words. While q is represented by c, x is shown as s at the beginning of a word and cs in the middle, and z is represented by s. U is used for a w at the beginning of a word.

cuaraidh – quarry

saidleafòn – xylophone

tacsaidh – taxi

sinc – zinc

uèir – wire

VARIATIONS IN PRONUNCIATION

As with other languages, there are varieties of Gaelic. The differences are marked enough to enable a seasoned listener to recognise a speaker as being from Argyll, Barra, Lewis or wherever. Although variations in vocabulary and accent may cause a little difficulty at first, all speakers can understand one another. Naturally, there is a certain amount of friendly debate as to which variety of Gaelic is best! But, as with good whisky, a 'blend' of them all is acceptable.

As well as differences in pronunciation, there are also variations in vocabulary between dialects. A common example of this is the expression for I like

is toigh leam   used in most dialects

is caomh leam   used mostly in Lewis dialects

Is caomh leam an còta agaibh!

O! Tapadh leibh... A bheil sibh à Leòdhas?

WORD ORDER

Gaelic has a different word order to English. In Gaelic, the verb normally comes first, then the subject, followed by the rest of the sentence.

tha mi fuar – I am cold

The above example is made up of the following parts:

tha   am (Present Tense)

mi   I

fuar   cold

Here are some examples of this word order:

tha an gille beag – The boy is small.

tha mi a' fuireach ann an Glaschu –
   I am living in Glasgow or I live in Glasgow.

tha i fuar an-diugh – It is cold today.

The main exceptions to this are the question words **càit**, **ciamar**, **cò**, **cuin**, and **dè** which always appear at the beginning of the sentence. For example:

ciamar a tha sibh? – How are you?

càit a bheil sibh a' fuireach? –
   Where do you live?

NAMES

Throughout the Study Pack, you'll have noticed that changes often occur in people's names when they are addressed directly, or when someone else is calling them:

Màiri changes to **a Mhàiri**
Calum changes to **a Chaluim**

There's no strict rule over what to do with non-Gaelic names. Occasionally people do change them:

Bill changes to **a Bhill**
Carol changes to **a Charol**

but often these are left as they are.

When using the words **Mamaidh** and **Dadaidh**, most people change **Mamaidh** to **a Mhamaidh**, but leave **Dadaidh** unchanged – **Dadaidh**.

... a Mhamaidh ... Dadaidh...

BI – THE VERB TO BE

The most common forms of the verb To be in the Present Tense are:

tha

chan eil

a bheil?

tha is used to make positive statements e.g.

tha mi trang – I am busy

Tha mi trang!

chan eil is used to make negative statements e.g.

chan eil mi trang – I am not busy

Chan eil mi trang!

a bheil is used to ask questions e.g.

a bheil sibh trang? – Are you busy?

A bheil sibh trang?...

F HOW DOES THE LANGUAGE WORK? CIAMAR A THA AN CÀNAN AG OBRACHADH?

70

MASCULINES AND FEMININES

Gaelic nouns are either masculine or feminine. However, not everything female is feminine and not everything male is masculine. That's not how it works!

Girl – **nighean** for instance, is "feminine".

Woman – **boireannach** on the other hand, is "masculine".

When a word is "feminine", the following adjective is lenited, i.e. you add an 'h' after the first consonant, e.g.

nighean mhath – a good girl

madainn mhath – good morning

but when a word is masculine, the following adjective does not change.

feasgar math – Good afternoon / evening

This might seem complicated, but rest assured that practice does make perfect … eventually!

Here are the genders of some of the words you have met so far:

MASCULINE

feasgar	ospadal
siùcar	eilean
ainm	banca
saor	cofaidh
duine	bus
dràibhear	bainne
mac	balach
iasgair	sùgh
rathad	cupa

FEMININE

fàilte	obair
madainn	nurs
bean	oifis
eaglais	sgoil
fòn	cabhag
sràid	telebhisean
tì	trèan
mathair	oidhche
slàinte	àireamh
nighean	

A, AN AND THE

There is no word for 'a' or 'an' in Gaelic. So:

duine – man, or a man

latha – day, or a day

taigh-òsda – hotel, or an hotel

The most common form of 'the' in Gaelic is **an**:

an duine – the man

an latha – the day

an cofaidh – the coffee

For masculine words beginning with **b, f, m,** or **p,** however, you use **am** for 'the':

am baile – the town

am feasgar – the afternoon / evening

am mac – the son

am peann – the pen

There are other forms of 'the' which will be explained later in the course.

YES AND NO

Gaelic has no single equivalents to the English words yes and no. Instead, there are different ways of expressing a positive or a negative response. These depend on the question being asked.

To answer yes to a question beginning

a bheil …?

you say

tha.

To answer no, you say

chan eil.

In most other cases you respond with a form of the verb used in the question. For example

an toigh leibh cofaidh? – do you like coffee?

is toigh l' – yes (I like)

cha toigh l' – no (I don't like)

Now that you've worked your way through Study Pack 1, why not try out some of these other **Speaking Our Language** *materials?*

STUDY PACK 2...

carries on from this first pack and follows Programmes 10-18 of the TV series. You'll find the same combination of information and entertainment for all the family.

TAPES...

provide an opportunity to *hear* Gaelic spoken in all sorts of situations and help you to build up your confidence in pronouncing new words. Speaking Our Language tapes come in sets of three, covering the same ground as the whole of the first series. The tapes have been designed to be used without reference to a textbook, so they are ideal for use in your car.

VIDEOS...

will give you a chance to recap on the television programmes. Set 1 incorporates Programmes 1-9 while Set 2 covers Programmes 10-18.

WANT TO KNOW MORE?

Our free information service could help you if you want to know more about learning Gaelic. We will be keeping details of Gaelic classes and activities all over Scotland. Ring us at the number below!

AFTER THE PROGRAMME...

Keep in touch through Speaking Our Language newsletters. The first issue is available in May 1993.

Please contact us at the address or phone number below if you would like to order any of the items listed, or if you would like further information. We'd also like to hear how you're getting on with learning through Speaking Our Language, so why not drop us a line?

Cànan
P.O. Box 345,
Isle of Skye
IV44 8XA

Tel: 04714 345   **Fax: 04714 322**